CAMBRIDGE
SELF HINDI TEACHER

CAMBRIDGE
SELF HINDI TEACHER

Prof. P.S. Bhatnagar
M.A. L.L.B
Former Member Executive & Research
Committee (I.C.W.A)
(Thirty Years of Teaching Experience)
Revised and Edited by

Pradeep Chhabra
B.Com
(Twenty Years of Teaching Experience)

Pankaj Publications
New Delhi

© PUBLISHERS
First Print 1985.
Revised Edition 2001
ISBN No. : 81-87155-10-8

Published by :
Pankaj Publications
For **Cambridge Book Depot**
3, Regal Building, Sansad Marg,
New Delhi-110 001
Phone : 336 3395, 3348805
Telefax : 91-11-5546260
Email : cambridgebooks@hotmail.com

Laser Typesetting by
Sunrise Graphics
Email : chandhok54@hotmail.com

A Word to the Tourists

It was on my return journey from Bombay to Delhi that I had an opportunity of a free and frank discussion witha group of European Tourists. In the course of my conversation, I came to know of certain problems faced by foreigners in India. The major hurdle was language specially for visitors from France, Germany and other European countries. They are not acquainted with English. Their first effort is to familiarise themselves with Hindi and acquire its workable knowledge. They told me that most of the books written for the purpose were loaded with grammar, its rules and functions whereas the tourist is more interested and badly needs a book that could introduce him to conversational aspects of language.

Therefore, after a detailed talk on the subject and taking note of the difficulties experienced not only by Europeons but also by many Asians and even Indians from non-Hindi regions that I prepared an outline to suit their aims and put that in the form of the book.

While saying a word to the learner, specially to 'The Tourists', I wish to communicate the following important points to facilitate their approach and understanding of the language which is spoken in India by a large majority. Its roots are deep and well spread out. In fact it is a child grown into youth after being nourished and nurtured by ancient Indian classical and common people's languages like Sankrit, Pali, Prakrit, Braj Bhasha and Khariboli. Even Persian langauge has contributed much to its development. Amir Khusro, a Persian, was the first great initiator and promoter of the language almost seven centuries ago. Abdur-Rahim khan-e-khana, Kabir, Tulsidas and many eminent saint-scholars gave life and meaning to it.

In this brief attempt, specially for those who are keen to familiarize themselves with it within few days time, all grammatical complicaitons have been avoided and a direct approach made to make the learner know correct poronunciation, construction of short sentences and essential vocabulary, so that tourists or other persons interested in acquiring sufficient knowledge of basic principles of Hindi may not feel any difficulty in communicaiton with the people here in India.

Important things stressed here are : Correct knowledge of Alphabets, word formation, pronunciation-making out of short conversatinal sentences likely to be spoken in every day on common occasions. It is a fact that it is not difficult to learn Hindi. Any person deciding to know it can do so in a week's time. The problem however, is in writing where a learner commits errors in placing correct vowel signs in conjuction with consonants; hence this aspect is dealt with greater stress.

All the care has also been taken of maintaining the standard of language, style and contents to best serve the purpose.

Having met large number of Indian and Foreign Tourists to North India, I came to know of their problems of communication. Therefore, after inviting their suggestions, I ventured to prepare this brief but purposeful book for their convenience.

On my part, I believe, the learners will find it useful in preparing for getting through the intended Hindi conversations. Wishing best of luck!

AUTHOR

CONTENTS

Page

PART I

PART II

PART I

Chapter 1
Hindi Alphabet

The Hindi alphabet has sixteen vowels and thirty six consonants. We shall deal with vowels first.

स्वर
(VOWELS)

अ	आ	इ	ई
A	AA(Ā)	I	EE(Ī)
उ	ऊ	ए	ऐ
U	OO(Ū)	E	AI
ओ	औ	अं	अः
O	AU	AN:	AH*
ऋ*	ॠ**	ऌ*	ॡ**
RI	REE	LRI	LREE

These are sixteen vowels. We have given alongside the equivalent English letter or letters which we have used in this book to indicate the pronunciation. The Hindi vowels marked with two asterisks are never used and so may be safely omitted from study. Those marked with one asterisk are rarely used.

1

व्यंजन
(CONSONANTS)

क	ख	ग	घ	ड.
KA	KHA	GA	GHA	NG
च	छ	ज	झ	ञ
CHA	CHHA	JA	JHA	NY
ट	ठ	ड	ढ	ण
ṬA	ṬHA	ḌA	ḌHA	ṆA
त	थ	छ	ध	न
TA	THA	DA	DHA	NA
प	फ	ब	भ	म
PA	PHA	BA	BHA	MA
य	र	ल	व	श
YA	RA	LA	VAorWA	SHA
ष	स	ह		
SHA	SA	HA		
क्ष	त्र	ज्ञ		
KSHA	TRA	GYA		

These are thirty six consonants. A consonant without vowel sound is difficult to pronounce, so the consonants given above include the short sound of **a**. For example क has in fact the sound of **k** and and short a.

If we want the pure consonants sound of **k** without **a** we should write क् i.e. we should put a stroke (हलन्त) under it. But the Hindi consonants are generally written without strokes under them. The consonants **ng** (ङ) and **ny** (ञ) are not used independently, but are compounded with other consonants.

Note : अ is also written as ञ्र.

ण is also written as राा.

भ is also written as झ.

Hindi Consonants with a dot under them

In Hindi, we put dots under some consonants. This changes the pronunciation of the consonants.

(i)   If a dot is put under ड (d) to read ड़, the letter has a sound between d and r. This sound is absent in English, we have indicated it by **d**.

(ii) If a dot is put under ढ (dh) to read ढ़, the letter has a sound between **dh** and **rh**. This sound is absent in English. We have indicated it by **dh**.

(iii) If a dot is put under ख (kha) to read ख़, it becomes more aspirate. There is no corresponding sound in English. This letter ख़ generally occurs in Urdu words, which have been absorbed in Hindi. In pure Hindi words, this sound is absent.

3

(iv) If a dot is put under ज (j) to read as ज़, it acquires the sound of **z** as in zoo, zeal. This ज़ is also used is Urdu words absorbed in Hindi and is absent in pure Hindi words.

(v) If a dot is put under फ (ph) to read as फ़, it acquires the sound of **f** in English as in feel, friend etc. This is also an importation from Urdu and is absent in Hindi.

There are some words in Hindi, wherein there is **not** the full sound of 'n' but only a partial nasal sound of 'n' as in French words. These have been indicated by the mark **n:**. In Hindi this is written as i.e. a crescent and a dot on top.

Particular attention of the readers is invited to the following groups of letters where the same English letters have been used to denote the hard and the soft sounds, with the distinction that to indicate the hard sound of t,d,n we have used dot under them, but for indicating the soft sound the Roman type has been used

Thus:

Hard sound	*Soft Sound*
ट ṭa	त ta
ठ ṭha	थ tha
ड ḍa	छ da
ढ ḍha	घ dha
ण na	न na

4

Readers are requested to watch how persons, whose mother tongue is Hindi, pronounce the Hindi words. That would be of great assistance in picking up the correct prouanciation. Those who have no opportunity to mix with Hindi speaking people, may with benefit hear the broadcasts in Hindi.

अब	(ab)	now
आम	(am)	mango
इस	(is)	this
इन	(in)	these
उस	(us)	that
उन	(un)	those
ऊन	(un)	wool
एक	(ek)	one

EXERCISE FOR READING

अ	आ	इ	ई
उ	ऊ	ए	ऐ
ओ	औ	अं	अः

5

After you have grasped all examples, try the following words :

अब	आज	इस	ईख
ab	āj	is	īkh
उस	ऊन	एक	ऐनक
us	ūn	ek	ainak
ओखली	औरत	अंगीठी	अ:
okhali	aurat	angithi	ah:
अनार	आम	इमली	ईंट
anār	ām	imalī	īt
उस्तरा	ऊंट	एकल	ऐसा
ustrā	ūnt	ekal	aisā
ओठ	औजार	अंगूठी	
oth	aujār	angūthī	

Sound of 'a' as in normal, formal; 'a' as in father, car; 'i' as in hit, sit; 'i' as in Delhi, machine,; 'u' as in bull, full; 'u' in crucible, crucial; e as in they, pet, red; 'ai' as in said; 'o' as in got, shot, so; 'o' as in moon, fool; 'au' as in audit, Paul.

6

Chapter 2

Combining the Vowel Sound of आ Ā (AA) with Consonants

In Hindi one vertical line in put, to blend with the consonant the long sound of a, as per pronounced in grass, father, para etc.

Thus क ka becomes का kaa (kā); ग ga becomes गा ga; म ma becomes मा mā; र ra becomes का rā and so on.

EXERCISE FOR READING

का	खा	गा	घा	ङ
चा	छा	जा	झा	ञ
टा	ठा	डा	ढा	ण

You have now learnt how to combine the vowel **a** with a consonant and can easily read the following :

खाना	(khānā)	**food**
गाना	(gānā)	**singing**
जाना	(jānā)	**to go**
पान	(pān)	**a betel leaf**

7

काम	(kām)	work
खाना	(khānā)	to eat
गान	(gān)	a song
लाना	(lānā)	to bring
लड़ना	(larnā)	to fight
मामा	(māmā)	maternal uncle
नाना	(nānā)	mother's father
सारा	(sārā)	whole
झाग	(jhāg)	foam
मान	(mān)	respect
राग	(rāg)	melody
भाग	(bhāg)	division
नाग	(nāg)	serpent
सास	(sās)	mother-in-law
राम	(Rām)	Hindi God
साग	(sāg)	leafy vegetables

Chapter 3

Combining the Vowel Sounds of इ (I) and ई (I) with Consonants

In English **i** or **I** is put afte the consonant to give it the vowel sound of **i** as in hit, sit, kit or to blend the vowel sound of **ee** as in meet, been, keen etc. In Hindi इ or ई is used independently when the vowel is not combined with any consonant but when the vowel sound of **i** is combined with a consonant, a small vertical line with a loop ि is is prefixed to combine the vowel sound of **i** with the consonant. Thus we write :

हिट (hit), किल (kill),   हिम (him) etc.

EXERCISE FOR READING

कि	पि	चि	ति
खि	फि	छि	थि
गि	बि	जि	दि
घि	भि	झि	धि

Notice that in each of the above, a vertical line and a loop above is put to blend the vowel sound of **i** with the consonant.

But when we want to blend the vowel sound of **ee(ी)**, the vertical line and the loop are suffixed. Thus a vertical line and a loop on top ी is the symbol to impart the sound of **ee (ī)**. If the vowel sound of ee(ī) is to be pronounced independently as in **फील (feel)**, the letter **ई** is written saparately.

Exercise for reading

की	पी	ची	ती
खी	फी	छी	थी
गी	बी	जी	दी

After you have mastered reading above, try the following words:

हिट	सिट	किन	किथ	लिड	निब
hīt	sīt	kīn	kīth	līd	nīb
पिन	रिब	सिन	किस	किल	टिन
pīn	rīb	sīn	kīsh	kīll	tīn
विम	हिज	हिम	लिट	किट	सिप
vīm	hīs	hīm	līt	kīt	sīp

It will be seen that the difference in the symbols ि and ी is that former is put on the left hand side of a letter while the latter is put on the right side.

मीट	सीप	रील	कीप	पील	नीड
meet	seep	reel	keep	peel	need
रीड	सी	सीड	सीम	सीक	सील
reed	see	seed	seem	seek	seel
बीन	कीन	फील	फी	हील	सीन
been	keen	feel	fee	heel	seen

Chapter 4

Combining the Vowel Sounds of उ (U) and ऊ (OO) or (Ū) with Consonants

When the vowel sound of उ (u) is used independently the letter उ is used. But when it has to be blended with a consonant, a small hook-like symbol is put under the consonant.

EXERCISE FOR READING

कु	खु	गु	घु
चु	जु	जु	झु
टु	ठु	डु	ढु
पु	फु	बु	भु

(ु) symbol to denote short उ (u).

There is one exception to this rule. When we have to write **ru**, we do not put a hook-like symbol under र but we write **ru** as रु.

When we have to blend the sound of **oo (ū)**, we put symbol of ू below the consonant, but when we have to put it to र (**ra**) we put it in the middle. (ू) symbol to denote long ऊ (ū).

कू	खू	गू	घू
चू	छू	जू	झू
पू	फू	बू	भू

11

Now read the following :

कुर्सी	खुशी	गुलाब	पुकारना
kursī	khushī	gulāb	pukārnā
chair	happiness	rose	to call loudly
सुनना	दुकान	मुस्कराना	पुराना
sunanā	dukān	muskarānā	purānā
to hear	a shop	to smile	old (wornout)
नुकसान	सुख	रूपया	रूकना
nukasān	sukh	rupayā	rukanā
harm, damage	comfort, happiness	rupees, money	to stop, to stay

The symbol (ꠖ) is joined to letters as shown below:

फूल	phūl	flower
सूखा	sūkhā	dry
पूरा	pūrā	full, complete
कूड़ा	kūrā	rubbish, dirt
थूकना	thūkanā	to spit
चूमना	chūmanā	to kiss
लूटना	lūtanā	to loot, to plunder
डाकू	dākū	a dacoit
रूप	rūp	beauty, appearance
झाड़ू	jhārū	a broom

12

Chapter 5

Combining the Vowel Sounds of ए (E) and ऐ (AI) with Consonants

When the vowel sound of ए (e) and ऐ (ai) are not blended with any consonant, they are written separately as above, but when they are compunded with any consonant the following symbols are added to the consonant.

for ए put one slanting stroke on top (`).

EXERCISE FOR READING

के	खे	गे	घे
चे	छे	जे	भे
ते	थे	दे	धे
ने	पे	फे	बे

For adding the vowel sound of ऐ (ai) two slanting strokes (˝) are added on top.

कै	खै	गै	घै
पै	फै	बै	भै
मै	यै	रै	लै

These symbols are added as shown above.

Now Read the following words :

एक	ek	one
केला	kelā	a banana

खेल	khel	a play
सेब	seb	an apple
तेल	tel	oil
मेला	melā	fair
जेल	jel	a jail, imprisonment

Note : Here (ai) has the same sound as 'a' has in हैज 'has', हैड 'had', हैन्ड 'hand' etc.

मैला	melā	dirty
कैसा ?	kaisa?	of which kind?
कैसे ?	kaise?	how?
कै	kai	vomitting
फैलाना	phailanā	to spread out
तैरना	tairanā	to swim
पैसा	paisā	money
है	hai	is
ऐसा	aisā	of this kind

Sound of 'a' as in normal, formal; 'a' as in father, car, 'i' as in hit, sit; 'i' as in Delhi, machine; 'u' as in bull, full; 'u' as in crucible, crucial; e as in they, pet, red; 'ai' as in said; 'o' as in got, shot, so; 'o' as in moon, fool; 'au' as in audit, Paul.

Chapter 6

Combining the Vowel Sounds of ओ (O) and औ (AU) with Consonants

These vowels when not compounded with any consonants are written as above but when integrated with a consonant, the symbol of a vertical line infront and slanting stroke on top (ो) is used

EXERCISE FOR READING

को	खो	गो	घो
टो	ठो	डो	ढो
पो	फो	बो	भो
मो	यो	रो	लो

To combine the vowel sound of औ (au), a vertical line infornt and two slanting strokes on top (ौ) are added to the consonant.

कौ	खौ	गौ	घौ
चौ	छौ	जौ	झौ
पौ	फौ	बौ	भौ
मौ	यौ	रौ	लौ

You have now leant how to combine the vowels with a consonant and can easily read the following:

कोई	koī	some one
कोना	konā	a corner
जो	jo	who, whoever, whatever
रोना	ronā	to cry, to weep
होना	honā	to be
मोर	mor	a peacock
धोना	dhonā	to wash
तोता	totā	a parrot
सोचना	sochanā	to think

The symbol (ौ) is added as shown below :

कौन ?	kaun?	who?
कौआ	kauā	a crow
नौकर	naukar	a servant
पौना	paunā	three quarters
चौथा	chauthā	one fourth
मौसम	mausam	the weather
लौटना	lautanā	to return
जौ	jau	barley

Chapter 7

Combining the Vowel Sounds of अं (AN) with Consonants

When अं (an) does not combine with a consonant it is written separately as in : अंडा, अंडर

But when the vowel is compounded with a consonant, a small zero is put on the top of the preceding consonant.

ठंडा	ṭhandā	cold
मंडी	mandī	a local market
टंडन	ṭandan	a surname
डंडा	ḍanḍa	a thick short
दंड	danḍ	punishment
रंग	rang	colour

EXERCISE FOR READING

कं	खं	गं	घं
पं	फं	बं	भं
मं	यं	रं	लं

The small zero is also put along with other vowel symbols to indicate the sound of **n** when compounded with other vowels.

पिंक	pink	हैंड	hand
मौंक	monk	लैंड	land

लांड्री	laundry	सैंड	sand
सिंक	sink	रैंट	rant
सैंक	sank	पाउंड	pound
पैंट	pant	लौंग	long
संग	sang	रंग	rang
लंगर	langar	लंगूर	langūr
अंक	ank	रंक	rank
लंका	lankā	दंगा	danga
चंगा	changa	नंगा	nanga

Readers have now become familiar with symbol of dot or 'small cipher' on top which gives the nasal sound of 'an'.

When this nasal sound of 'an' is not full but pronounced only half of lightly, it is expressed by the sign (ँ) on top. The significance of putting a loop below the dot is that the sound of 'an' is not fully nasal but just a little nasal inflexion is given to the letter on which the sign in put.

Sound of 'a' as in normal, formal; 'a' as n father, car; 'i' as as in hit, sit; 'i' as in Delhi, machine; 'u' as in bull, full; 'u'' as in crucible, crucial; e as in they, pet, red; 'ai' as in said; 'o' as in got, shot, so; 'o' as in moon, fool; 'au' as in audit, Paul.

It would be a good exercise to write this combining the matras with consonant.

क k	का kā	कि ki	की kī	कु ku	कू kū	के ke	कै kai	को ko	कौ kau	कं kan	कः kah
ख kh	खा khā	खि khi	खी khī	खु khu	खू khū	खे khe	खै khai	खो kho	खौ khau	खं khan	खः khah
ग g	गा gā	गि gi	गी gī	गु gu	गू gū	गे ge	गै gai	गो go	गौ gau	गं gan	गः gah
घ gh	घा ghā	घि ghi	घी ghī	घु ghu	घू ghū	घे ghe	घै ghai	घो gho	घौ ghau	घं ghan	घः ghah

And so on this exercise would be of help particularly to those who are learning to read and write.

19

Chapter 8

Conjunct Consonant

Now you know how a vowel a combined with a consonant.

A number of words in Hindi have two consonants combined. In such a case the first consonant is written incompletely and joined with the second consonant. For example, if two क are combined :

क + क = क्क

Another way to joining two consonants is to add a stroke under the first letter. This may be easier until you have had a good practice in writing.

क + क = क़्क

But it would be helpful to know the first method also since while reading that is the more likely form of conjucts you will come across.

Consonants in Hindi are of two types :

(i) those which have a vertical line in the end, and

(ii) those which do not have a vertical line.

The following consonants come under the first type:

क	ख	ग	घ	च	ज	झ	ञ	ण	त
ध	न	प	फ	ब	भ	म	य	ल	व
श	ष	स	क्ष	त्र	ज्ञ				

The seond type :

छ ट ठ ड ढ र ह

A vowel is pronounced alone but a vowel sign pronounced together with a consonant. Each vowel represented with a sign. It is also shown how it is represented with a combined with a vowel.

Vowel	Sign of Matra with a consonant	as combined with	Example
अ	(a) has no vowel Sign as it is inherent in a consonant		
आ	(ā) ा	क + आ = का ka + ā = kā	काला kālā (black)
इ	(i) ि	क + ि = कि ka + ī = kī	किताब kitāb (book)
ई	(ī) ी	क + ी = की	कीमा kīmā (mince meat)
		ka + a = ka	
उ	(u) ु	क + ु = कु ka + ū = kū	कुरता kurtā (Indian shirt)
ऊ	(ū) ू	क + ू = कू ka + u = ku	कूद kūd (jump)
ए	(e) े	क + े = के ka + e = ke	केला kelā (banana)
ऐ	(ai) ै	क + ै = कै ka + ai = kai	कैसा kaisā (how)

21

ओ	(o) ो	क + ो = को	कोना konā
		ka + o = ko	(corner)
औ	(au) ौ	क + ौ = कौ	कौन kaun
		ka + au = kau	(who)?
अं	(ang) ं	क + अं = कं	कंघी kanghī
		ka + ang = kan	(comb)

Note : If the nasal sound comes in the end it will be mard (ं) e.g. kahan (कहां)

It would be a good exercise to write this out combing the **matras** with different consonants.

क and झ have a vertical line but they have a hook in the end. When combining them with another consonant, the hook is left midway so that it may be joined with the second letter.

क	+	क	=	क्क
क	+	व	=	क्व
झ	+	झ	=	झ्झ

ट, ठ, ड and ढ cannot be combined in either way. They are, therefore, joined to another consonant by adding a stroke under the first letter.

| ट | + | ट | = | ट्ट |
| ट | + | ड | = | ट्ड |

Sometimes these four letters mentioned above are combined like this :

22

$$\text{ट} \quad + \quad \text{ट} \quad = \quad \text{ट्ट}$$
$$\text{ट} \quad + \quad \text{ठ} \quad = \quad \text{ट्ठ}$$
$$\text{ड} \quad + \quad \text{ड} \quad = \quad \text{ड्ड}$$

But this way of writing is cumbersome and not attractive. It is better, therefore, to add a stroke to the first letter of the conjuct ट, ठ इ etc. Now a word about

कर्म	*Karma*	act, action
क्रम	*krama*	order, sequence
कृपा	*kripā*	kindness

1. In the first instance *karma, ra* comes before the last letter *ma,* and appears in the form of a hook on the top of the letter which follows it.

2. In the second example *krama, ra* is joined to the first consonant *ka,* and is in the form of a stroke under it.

3. In the third word *kripā, ra* and *i* are joined to *ka.* If *ra* is combined with *i* in a conjunct, it is symbolised s added under the consonant to which it is joined

23

Chapter 9

Exercise for Reading

The following exercise for reading is constituted of those words of English which are in current use in Hindi:

Exercise 1

Account	एकाउन्ट	Driver	ड्राइवर
Appeal	अपील	Engine	इन्जिन
Ball	बॉल	Express	एक्सप्रेस
Bag	बैग	Fees	फीस
Barrister	बैरिस्टर	File	फाइल
Bathroom	बॉथरूम	Gate	गेट
Bicycle	बाईसिकिल	Goal	गोल
Bill	बिल	Guard	गार्ड
Carbon	कार्बन	Head-master	हैडमास्टर
Cinema	सिनेमा	Holder	होल्डर
Car	कार	Jail	जेल
Club	क्लब	Judge	जज
Director	डायरेक्टर	Junction	जंक्शन
Doctor	डॉक्टर	Lamp	लैम्प

Late	लेट	Registry	रजिस्टरी
Late Fee	लेट फी	Seal	सील
Map	मैप	Seat	सीट
Manager	मैनेजर	Share	शेयर
Market	मार्किट	Signal	सिग्नल
Money Order	मनी आर्डर	Table	टेबिल
Packet	पैकेट	Tax	टेक्स
Pant	पैंट	Ticket	टिकिट
Paper	पेपर	Time	टाइम
Press	प्रेस	Type	टाइप
Programme	प्रोग्राम	Telephone	टेलिफोन
Racket	रैकेट	Wagon	वैगन
Rate	रेट	Waiting room	वैटिंग रूम
Rail	रेल	Watch	वाच
Rubber	रबर	War	वार
Radio	रेडियो	Wrist	रिस्ट
Register	रजिस्टर	Watch	वाच

Exercise 2

Shrimati Indira Gandhi	श्रीमति इन्दिरा गाँधी
Lal Bahadur Shastri	लाल बहादुर शास्त्री
Jawaharlal Nehru	जवाहर लाल नेहरू
Dr. Rajendra Prasad	डॉ0 राजेन्द्र प्रसाद
Dr. Zakir Hussain	डॉ0 जाकिर हुसैन
Swarn Singh	स्वर्ण सिंह
Morarji Desai	मोरारजी देसाई
Ch. Charan Singh	चौ0 चरण सिंह
Atal Behari Vajpayee	अटल बिहारी वाजपेई
Lakshmi	लक्ष्मी
Chintamani	चिन्ता मणी
Ambika	अम्बिका
Dwarka Prasad	द्वारका प्रसाद
Tyagaraja	त्यागराज
Rajiv Gandhi	राजीव गाँधी
Giani Zail Singh	ज्ञानी ज़ैल सिंह
Gautam Buddha	गौतम बृद्ध
Samrat Ashok	सम्राट अशोक

PART II

Parts of Human Body

ankle	टरखना	*takhanā (M)*
armpit	बगल	*bagal (F)*
arm	बाँह	*bānh (F)*
back	पीठ	*pīth (F)*
beard	दाढ़ी	*darhī (F)*
blood	खून	*khūn (M)*
body	शरीर	*sharār (M)*
bone	हड्डी	*haddī (F)*
brain	दिमाग	*dīmag (M)*
breast (woman's)	स्तन	*stan (M)*
cheek	गाल	*gāl (M)*
chest	छाती	*chhātī (F)*
chin	ठोड़ी	*thōdī (F)*
ear	कान	*kān (M)*
elbow	कोहनी	*kōhanī (F)*
eye	आँख	*ankh (F)*
eyeball	पुतली	*putlī (F)*

eyebrow	भौं	*bhāun (F)*
eyelashes	पलक	*palak (F)*
face	चेहरा	*chehrā (M)*
finger	अंगुली	*angulī (F)*
finger-nail	नाखून	*nākhun (M)*
flesh	माँस	*māns (M)*
foot	पैर	*Paīr (M)*
forehead	माथा	*mathā (M)*
hand	हाथ	*hāth (M)*
head	सिर	*Sīr (M)*
heard	दिल, हृदय	*dīl, hridaya (M),*
hair	बाल	*bāl (M)*
heel	एडी	*edī (F)*
kidney	गुर्दा	*gurdā (M)*
lip	होंठ	*hōth (M)*
liver	जिगर	*jīgar (M)*
lung	फेफड़ा	*phēpharā (M)*
moustache	मूँछ	*mūnchh M)*
mouth	मूँह	*mūnh (M)*
neck	गर्दन	*gardan (M)*

nose	नाक	*nāk (F)*
palm	हथेली	*hathelī(F)*
shoulder	कन्धा	*kandhā(M)*
skin	चमड़ी	*chamrī*
skull	खोपड़ी	*khōparī(F)*
spine	रीढ़	*reēd (M)*
stomach	पेट	*pet (M)*
teeth	दाँत	*dānt (M)*
thigh	जांघ	*jāngh (M)*
toe	पैर की अँगुली	*pāir-kī-angulī(F)*
tongue	जीभ	*jībh (F)*
throat	गला	*galā(M)*
thumb	अंगूठा	*anguthā(M)*
vein	नस	*nas (F)*
waist	कमर	*kamar (F)*
wrist	कलाई	*kalāī(F)*

Chapter 11
Animals

animal	जानवर	*jānvar (M)*
bear	भालू	*bhālū (F)*
buffalo	भैस, भैसा	*bhaĩs (M)* *bhaĩsā (M)*
bullock	बैल	*baīl (M)*
cat	बिल्ली	*billī (F)*
camel	ऊँट, ऊँटनी	*ūnt (M) ūntni (F)*
cow	गाय	*gāy (F)*
calf	बछड़ा, बछिया	*bachhrā (M)* *bachhiā (F)*
deer	हिरन	*hīran (M)*
dog	कुत्ता	*kuttā (M)*
bitch	कुतिया	*kutiā (F)*
donkey	गधा	*gadhā (M)*
elephant	हाथी, हथिनी	*hathī (M), hathnī (F)*
fox	लोमड़ी	*lōmrī (F)*
goat	बकरा, बकरी	*bakarā (M) bakarī (F)*

horse	घोड़ा	$gh\bar{o}r\bar{a}(M)$
mare	घोड़ी	$gh\bar{o}r\bar{\imath}(F)$
mule	टट्टू	$tatt\bar{u}(M)$
monkey	बदंर	$bandar\ (M)$
mouse	चूहा	$ch\bar{u}h\bar{a}(M)$
lamb	मेमना	$m\bar{e}mn\bar{a}(M\ \&\ F)$
lion	सिंह, बब्बर शेर	$s\bar{\imath}nha,\ bab\bar{a}r$ $sh\bar{e}r\ (M)$
lioness	सिंहनी	$s\bar{\imath}mhan\bar{\imath}(F)$
python	अजगर	$ajgar\ (M)$
snake	साँप	$s\bar{a}np$
sheep	भेड़	$bh\bar{e}r\ (F)$
skunk	छछुन्दर	$Chhachh\bar{u}ndar\ (M)$
squirrel	गिलहरी	$g\bar{\imath}lahr\bar{\imath}(F),$
tiger	शेर	$sh\bar{e}r\ (M)$
tigress	शेरनी	$sh\bar{e}rn\bar{\imath}(F)$

Birds

bat	चमगादड़	*Chamgādar (M)*
bird	पक्षी, चिड़िया	*pakshī, chīrīyā (M)*
crow	कौआ	*kōuā (M)*
cock	मुर्गा	*mūrgā (M)*
crane	सारस	*sāras (M)*
cuckoo	कोयल	*kōyal (F)*
duck	बत्तख	*batakh (F)*
hen	मुर्गी	*mūrgī (F)*
kite	चील	*chīl (F)*
nightingale	बुलबुल	*būlbūl (F)*
owl	उल्लू	*ullū (M)*
patridge	तीतर	*tītar (M)*
parrot	तोता	*tōtā*
peacock	मोर	*mōr (M)*
pigeon	कबूतर	*kabūtar (M)*
sparrow	गौरैया	*gaūraiyā (F)*
swan	हंस	*hans (M)*
vulture	गिद्ध	*gīddha (M)*

Fish and Water Animals

crab	केकड़ा	*kēkrā (M)*
crocodile	मगर	*magar (M)*
fish	मछली	*machhī (M)*
leech	जोंक	*jōnk (F)*
tortoise	कछुवा	*kachhuā (M)*

Insects

ant	चींटी	*chīntī (F)*
ant (white)	दीमक	*dīmak (F)*
bee	मधुमरखी	*madhūmakkhī (F)*
bug	खटमल	*khatmal (M)*
butterfly	तितली	*titlī (F)*
fly	मक्खी	*makkhi (F)*
frog	मेढक	*mēndhak (M)*
germs	किटाणु	*kitānu (M)*
glow worm	जुगनु	*juganu (M)*
insect	कीड़ा	*kīrā (M)*
lizard	छिपकली	*chhipkalī (F)*
locust	टिड्डी	*Tiddī (F)*
mosquito	मच्छर	*machchhar (M)*
scorpion	बिच्छू	*bichchhū (M)*
spider	मकड़ी	*makrī (F)*

33

Chapter 12

Food Stuff

English	Hindi	Transliteration
bread	रोटी	*rotī (F)*
butter	मक्खन	*makkan (M)*
butter-milk	छाछ	*chhāchh (M)*
cashewnut	काजू	*kāju (M)*
chicken	मुर्गी	*murgī (F)*
clarified butter	घी	*ghī (M)*
coconut (green)	नारियल	*nāriyal M)*
coconut (dry)	खोपरा	*khōprā (M)*
coffee	कॉफी	*kāufī (F)*
cottage cheese	पनीर	*panīr (M)*
corn	मक्का	*makkā (M)*
curd	दही	*dahī (M)*
dates	खजूर	*khajūr (F)*
dry fruit	मेवा	*meva (F)*
egg	अन्डा	*anda (M)*
fish	मछली	*machhalī (F)*
flour (whole wheat)	आटा	*ātā (M)*

34

flour (white)	मैदा	*maidā (F)*
gram	चना	*chanā (M)*
jaggery	गुड़	*gūr (M)*
lentils	दाल	*dāl (F)*
milk	दूध	*dūdh (F)*
oil	तेल	*tēl (M)*
pickle	अचार	*achār (M)*
rice	चावल	*chāval (M)*
salt	नमक	*namak (M)*
sugar	चीनी	*chīnī (F)*
wheat	गेहूँ	*gehūn (M)*

Vegetables

English	Hindi	Transliteration
beans (green)	सेम	*sēm (F)*
beans (string)	लोबिया	*lōbiyā (F)*
beans (French)	फरासबीन	*farāsbēan (F)*
cabbage	बन्द गोभी	*band gōbhī (F)*
carrot	गाजर	*gājar (F)*
cauliflower	फूल गोभी	*phul gōbhi (F)*
coriander (green)	हरा धनिया	*harā dhaniā (M)*
cucumber	खीरा	*khīrā (M)*
eggplant	बैंगन	*baingan (M)*
garlic	लहसुन	*lahsūn (M)*
lime, lemon	नीबू	*nību (M)*
mint	पुदिना	*pūdinā (M)*
onion	प्याज	*pyāz (F)*
okra	भिन्डी	*bhindī (F)*
peas	मटर	*matar (F)*
pepper (green)	शिमला मिर्च	*shimlā mirch (F)*
potato	आलू	*alū (M)*
pumpkin (red)	कद्दू	*kaddū (M)*
radish	मूली	*mūlī (M)*
spinach	पालक	*pālak (M)*
sweet potato	शकरकन्दी	*shakarkandī (F)*
tomato	टमाटर	*tamātar F)*
turnip	शलगम	*shalgam (F)*

Fruits

apple	सेब	*seb (M)*
apricot	खुमानी	*khumānī (F)*
banana	केला	*kelā (F)*
custard apple	शरीफ़ा	*shrīfā (M)*
grapes	अंगूर	*angūr (M)*
guava	अमरूद	*amrud (M)*
mango	आम	*ām (M)*
melon	खरबूजा	*kharbazā (M)*
orange	सन्तरा	*santarā (M)*
papaya	पपीता	*papeta (M)*
peach	आडू	*adū (M)*
pear	नाशपाती	*nāshpatū (M)*
pineapple	अनन्नास	*anannās (M)*
pomegranate	अनार	*anār (M)*
watermelon	तरबूज	*tarbūz (M)*

Spices and Condiments

aniseed	सौंफ	*sa ūnf (M)*
asafoatida	हींग	*hīng (F)*
bayleaf	तेजपात	*tejpat (M)*
cardamon (white)	छोटी इलायची	*choŏti elaichē (F)*
cardamon (black)	बडी इलायची	*badē elāichē (F)*
chillies (red)	लाल मिर्च	*lāl mirch (F)*
cinnamon	दालचीनी	*dalchīmī (F)*
cloves	लौंग	*laūng (M)*
coriander	धनिया	*dhaniyā (M)*
cumin	ज़ीरा	*zīrā (M)*
fenugreek	मेथी	*mēthī (F)*
garlic	लहसुन	*lahsūn (F)*
ginger	अदरक	*adrakh (F)*
mace	जावित्री	*jāvitri (F)*
mint	पुदिना	*pūdinā (M)*
mustard	राई	*rāi (F)*
nutmeg	जायफल	*jāyaphal (M)*
pepper (green)	हरी मिर्च	*hari mirch (F)*

pepper (black)	काली मिर्च	*kālī mirch (F)*
saffron	केसर	*kesar (F)*
salt	नमक	*namak (M)*
sesame	तिल	*til (M)*
spice	मसाला	*masālā (M)*
tamarind	इमली	*imlī (M)*
turmeric	हल्दी	*haldī (F)*

Foodgrains

barley	जौ	*jaū(M)*
flour	आटा	*āṭā (M)*
grain	अन्न	*anna* (M)
gram	चना	*chanā(M)*
gram flour	बेसन	*bēsan (M)*
kly (black)	उड़द	*urad (M)*

Weights and Measures

kilogram	किलोग्राम	*kilogrām (M)*
gram	ग्राम	*grām (M)*
scale	तराजू	*tarāzu (F)*
weight	वज़न	*vazan (M)*
heavy	भारी	*bhārī (ad)*
light	हल्का	*halkā (ad)*
litre	लिटर	*litre (M)*
measurement	नाप	*nāp (M)*
metre	मीटर	*mātar (M)*
half	आधा	*ādhā (M)*
one quarter	एक -चौथाई	*ek chauthāī*
one third	एक -तिहाई	*ek-tihāī*
three quarters	तीन -चौथाई	*teēn - chauthāī*
to add	जोड़ना	*jōrnā*
to subtract	घटाना	*ghatanā*
to multiply	गुणा करना	*gūnā karnā*
to divide	भाग करना	*bhāg karnā*
beam	डंडी	*dandī*
pan	पलड़ा	*palarā*
counterpoise	धड़ा	*dharā*

Coins

rupee	रूपया	*rupayā*
pice	पैसा	*paisā*

Minerals, Metals and Precious Stones

mineral	खनिज	*khanji (M)*
metal	धातु	*dhātu (F)*
precious stone	रत्न	*ratna (M)*
brass	पीतल	*pītal (M)*
bronze	कांसा	*kansā (M)*
copper	तांबा	*tambā (M)*
gold	सोना	*sonā (M)*
silver	चाँदी	*chandī (F)*
steel	इस्पात	*ispāt (M)*
alum	फिटकरी	*phitkarī (F)*
chalk	खड़िया	*khariyā (F)*
clay	मिट्टी	*mittī (F)*
glass	शीशा	*shīshā (M)*
iron	लोहा	*lohā (M)*
lime	चूना	*chūnā (M)*
marble	संगमरमर	*sangmarmar (M)*
mercury	पारा	*pārā (M)*
coral	मूंगा	*mūngā (M)*
diamond	हीरा	*hīrā (M)*

emerald	पन्ना	*pannā (M)*
pearl	मोती	*motī (M)*
ruby	लाल मानिक	*lāl mānik (M)*
sapphire (blue)	नीलम	*nīlam (M)*
topaz	पुखराज	*pūkharaj (M)*
lead	सीसा	*sīsā (M)*
aluminium	अल्युमीनियम	*alūminīum (M)*

Chapter 13

Around the House

basket	टोकड़ी	*tŏkarī(M)*
bathroom	गुसलखाना	*gusalkhānā(M)*
bed	पलंग	*palang(M)*
bedcover	पलंगपोश	*palangpōsh (M)*
bedsheet	चादर	*chādar (M)*
bottle	बोतल	*bōtal (F)*
bucket	बाल्टी	*bāltī(F)*
candle	मोमबत्ती	*mōmbattī(F)*
carpet	कालीन, गलीचा	*kālīn, galīchā*
ceiling	छत	*chhat (F)*
chair	कुर्सी	*kūrsī(F)*
comb	कंघा, कंघी	*kanghā, kanghī(M)*
cupboard	अलमारी	*almārī(F)*
curtain	पर्दा	*pardā(M)*
dining room	खाने का कमरा	*khanē kā kamarā(M)*
dining table	खाने की मेज़	*khāne kī mēz (F)*

divan	दिवान	*divān (M)*
drawing room	बैठक	*bathak (M)*
floor	फर्श	*farsh (F)*
floor rug	कालीन	*kālīm (F)*
guest room	मेहमान का कमरा	*mehmān kā kamarā (M)*
kitchen	रसोई	*rasoi (F)*
key	चाबी	*chābī (F)*
lock	ताला	*tālā (M)*
mattress	गद्दा	*gaddā (M)*
mat	चटाई	*chatāi (F)*
mirror	शीशा	*shīshā*
needle	सुई	*sūi (F)*
pillow	तकिया	*takiyā (M)*
scissors	कैंची	*kainchī (F)*
sieve	छलनी	*chhalanī (F)*
strainer	छन्नी	*chhannī (F)*
study	पढ़ने का कमरा	*parhne kā kamarā (M)*
soap	साबुन	*sābūn (M)*

table (writing)	लिखने की मेज	*likhane kī mez (F)*
thread	धागा	*dhāgā (M)*
umbrella	छाता, छतरी	*chhātā, chhatarī (F)*
utensils	बरतन	*bartan (M)*
varandah	बरामदा	*barāmadā (M)*
wall	दीवार	*dīvār (F)*
window	खिड़की	*khirki (F)*

Around the Town

airport	हवाई अड्डा	*havāī addā (M)*
building	इमारत	*imārat (F)*
bullock cart	बैलगाड़ी	*bailgārī (F)*
church	गिरजाघर	*girjāghar (M)*
college	कालिज	*college (M)*
crowd	भीड़	*bhīr (F)*
ditch	खाद, खाई	*khād, khāī (F)*
electricity	बिजली	*bijlī (F)*
farm	खेत, फारम	*khet, farm (M)*
fence	बाड़ा	*bārā (M)*
field	मैदान, खेत	*maidān, khet (M)*
garden	बाग, बगीचा	*bāg, bagīchā (M)*
gutter	नाला	*nālā (M)*
hawker	फेरीवाला	*pherīwālā (M)*
highway	बड़ी, सड़क	*bari sarak (F)*
hospital	अस्पताल	*aspatāl (M)*
hotel	होटल	*hotal (M)*
hut	झोंपड़ी	*jhonprī (F)*
inn	सराय	*sarāy (F)*

intersection (roads)	चौराहा	chaurāhā (M)
land	ज़मीन	zamīn (F)
lane	गली	galī (F)
library	पुस्तकालय	pustakālaya (M)
main market	बडा बाज़ार	barā bāzār (M)
market	बाज़ार	bāzār (M)
pole (electric)	बिजली का खम्भा	bijlī kā khambhā (M)
post	डाक	dāk (F)
postman	डाकिया	dākiyā (M)
post office	डाकघर	dākghar (M)
railway station	रेलवे स्टेशन	railway station (M)
restaurant	रेस्टोरेन्ट	restorent (M)
road	सड़क	sarak (F)
school	स्कूल	skūl (M)
sewage	नाला	nālā (M)
shop	दुकान	dukān (M)
shopkeeper	दुकानदार	dukāndār (M)
taxi	टैक्सी	taiksī (F)

48

telephone	टेलिफोन	*telifōn (M)*
telegraph office	तारघर	*tārghar (M)*
telegram	तार	*tār (M)*
university	विश्वविद्यालय	*vishvavidyāla (M)*
zoo	चिड़ियाघर	*chiriyāghar (M)*

Chapter 14

Trades and Professions

artisan	कारीगर	*karīgar (M & F)*
astrologer	ज्योतिषि	*jyotishi (M & F)*
author	लेखक, लेखिका	*lekhak, lekhikā (M & F)*
barber	नाई	*nāī (M)*
blacksmith	लुहार	*luhār (M)*
butcher	कसाई	*kasāī (M)*
carpenter	बढ़ई	*barhaī (M)*
cook	रसोइया, खानसामा	*rasoīyā, khānsamā*
dyer	रंगरेज	*rangrez (M)*
farmer	किसान	*kisān (M)*
gardener	माली	*mālī (M)*
goldsmith	सुनार	*sunār (M)*
jeweller	जौहरी	*jauharī (M)*
labourer	मजदूर	*mazdūr (M)*
merchant	व्यापारी	*vyāpārī (M)*
milkman	ग्वाला	*gvālā (M)*

nurse	नर्स	*nurse (F)*
potter	कुम्हार	*kumhār*
servant	नौकर	*naukar (M)*
servant (maid)	नौकरानी	*naukaranī(F)*
sweeper	जमादार	*jamādār (M)*
sweet vendor	हलवाई	*halwāi (M)*
printer	मुद्रक	*mūdrak (M)*
publisher	प्रकाशक	*prakāshak*
tailor	दर्जी	*darzī(M)*
teacher	शिक्षक	*chatai (F)*
teacher (lady)	शिक्षिका	*shikshikā*
washerman	धोबी	*dhobī(M)*
weaver	जुलाहा	*julāhā(M)*

Country and State

country	देश	*dēsh (M)*
native land	मातृभूमि	*mātribhūmi (F)*
state	प्रदेश	*pradesh (M)*
empire	साम्राज्य	*sāmrajya (M)*
kingdom	रियासत	*riyāsat (F)*
of Assam	आसामी	*Asami (M)*
of Bengal	बंगाली	*Bengālī (M)*
of Gujarat	गुजराती	*Gujāratī (M)*
of Kashmir	कश्मीरी	*Kashmīrī (M)*
of Madras	मद्रासी	*Madrāsī (M)*
of Maharashtra	मराठी	*Marāthī (M)*
of Marwar	मारवाड़ी	*Marwārī (M)*
of Nepal	नेपाली	*Nepālī (M)*
of Punjab	पंजाबी	*Punjābī (M)*
of Sindhi	सिन्धी	*Sindhī (M)*

Sound of 'a' as in nomral, formal; 'a' as in father, car; 'i' as in hit, sit; 'i' as in Delhi, machine; 'u' as in bull, full; 'u' as in crucible, crucial; e as in they, pet, red; 'ai' as in said; 'o' as in got, shot, so; 'o' as in moon, fool; 'au' as in audit, Paul.

Chapter 15

The Seasons

rainy season	बरसात	*barsāt(F)*
spring	बसंत	*basant (F)*
summer	गर्मी	*garmī(F)*
winter	जाड़ा	*jāṛā(M)*
rain	बारिश	*bārish (F)*
dust-storm	आंधी	*andhī(F)*
storm	तुफान	*tufān (F)*
wind	हवा	*havā(F)*
sun (heat)	धूप	*dhūp(F)*
chill	ठन्ड	*thand (F)*
heat	गर्मी	*garmī(F)*

Nature (prakriti)

air	हवा	*havā (F)*
atmosphere	वातावरण	*vātāvaran (M)*
breeze	हवा	*havā (F)*
cliff	चट्टान	*chattān (F)*
cloud	बादल	*bādal (M)*
current (river)	धारा	*dhārā (F)*
dawn	उषाकाल	*ushākāl (M)*
dark night	अन्धेरी रात	*andherī rāt (M)*
new moon	अमावस	*amāvas (M)*
dust	धूल	*dhūl (F)*
dust storm	आंधी	*andhī (F)*
earth	पृथ्वी	*prithvī (F)*
eclipse	ग्रहण	*grahān (M)*
fog	कोहरा	*kōhrā (M)*
hill	पहाड़ी	*phārī (F)*
hail	ओला	*olā (M)*
lake	झील	*jhīl (F)*
light (sun)	सूरज की रोशनी	*suraj kī rōshnī (F)*
moon	चाँद, चन्द्र	*chānd, chandra (M)*
moon (full)	पूर्ण चन्द्र	*purna chandra (M)*
moon light	चाँदनी	*chāndnī (F)*

54

moonlit night	चाँदनी रात	*chandnī rāt (F)*
full-moon night	पूर्णिमा	*purnimā (F)*
mountain	पहाड़	*pahār (M)*
ocean	महासागर	*mahāsāgar (M)*
peninsula	प्रायद्वीप	*prayādvīp (M)*
rain	बारिश	*bārish (F)*
rainbow	इन्द्रधनुष	*indradhanush (M)*
rainwater	बारिश का पानी	*bārish kā pānī (M)*
rainy season	बरसात	*barsāt (F)*
rainy day	बरसात का दिन	*barsāt kā din (M)*
rock	चट्टान	*chattān (F)*
sand	बालू	*bālu (F)*
sea	समुद्र	*samundra (M)*
seaside	समुद्र का किनारा	*samundra kā kinārā (M)*
sky	आसमान, आकाश	*asmān, akāsh (M)*
snow	बर्फ	*barf (F)*
star	तारा	*tārā (M)*
storm	तूफान	*tūfān (F)*
wave	लहर	*lahar (F)*
wind	हवा	*hava (F)*

Chapter 16

Politics, Government, etc.

administration	प्रशासन	*prashāsan (M)*
administrator	प्रशासक	*prashāsak (M & F)*
ambassador	राजदूत	*rājdūt (M & F)*
democracy	लोकतन्त्र	*lōktantra (M)*
diplomat	राजनयिक	*rājnayik (M & F)*
election	चुनाव	*chunāv (M)*
embassy	राजदूतावास	*rājdutāvās (M)*
federation	संघ	*sangh (M)*
federal	संघीय	*sanghīya (M)*
franchise	मताधिकार	*matādhikār (M)*
government	सरकार	*sarkār (F)*
governmental	सरकारी	*sarkārī (F)*
independence	स्वाधीनता	*svādhīnta (F)*
imprisonment	कैद	*quid (F)*
jail	जेल	*jail (M)*
judge	न्यायधीश	*nyāyadhīsh*
judgement	फैसला	*faislā (M)*

justice	न्याय	*nyāy (M)*
law	कानून	*kānun (M)*
law court	अदालत	*adālat (F)*
lawyer	वकील	*vakīl (M & F)*
law suit	मुकदमा	*mukadamā (M)*
legal	कानूनी	*kānunī (ad)*
municipality	नगरपालिका	*nagarpālikā (F)*
parliament	संसद	*sansad (M)*
parliment house	संसद भवन	*sansad bhawan (M)*
parliament member	संसद सदस्य	*sansad sadasya (M)*
politics	राजनीति	*rājnīti (F)*
political	राजनीतिक	*rājnītik*
politician	राजनीतिज्ञ	*rājnītigya (M & F)*
vote	मत	*mat (M)*
independence day	स्वाधीनता दिवस	*svādhinatā divas (M)*
republic day	गणतंत्र दिवस	*ganatantra divas (M)*
national flag	राष्ट्रीय झंडा	*rāshtriyā jhandā (M)*

High Offices in the Country

president	राष्ट्रपति	*rāshtrapati (M & F)*
vice-president	उपराष्ट्रपति	*upa-rāshtrapati (M & F)*
minister	मंत्री	*mantrī (M & F)*
minister of state	राज्यमंत्री	*rājya-mantrī (M & F)*
deputy minister	उपमंत्री	*upa-mantri (M & F)*
secretary (to govt.)	सचिव	*sachiva (M & F)*
governor	राज्यपाल	*rājyapāl*
president's house	राष्ट्रपति भवन	*rāshtrapati bhavan*
supreme court	सर्वोच्च न्यायालय	*sarvochcha nyāyalāya*
chief justice	मुख्य न्यायाधीश	*mukhya nyāyadhīsh*
cabinet	मंत्री मंडल	*mantrī mandal*
army	सेना	*senā (F)*
soldier	सैनिक	*sainik (M)*
to fight	लड़ाई करना	*larāī karnā*
war	युद्ध	*yuddha (M)*

peace	शान्ति	*shānti (F)*
weapon	हथियार	*hathiyār (M)*
gun	बन्दूक	*bandūk (F)*
bomb	बम	*bam (M)*
truce	संधी	*sandhī (F)*

Chapter 17

Fine Art, Literature, etc.

actor	अभिनेता	*abhinetā (M)*
actress	अभिनेत्री	*abhinetrī (F)*
art	कला	*kalā (F)*
artist	कलाकार	*kalākār (M & F)*
audience	दर्शक	*darshak (M)*
dance	नाच, नृत्य	*nāch, nritya (M)*
dancer	नर्तक, नर्तकी	*nartak (M), nartakī (F)*
drama	नाटक	*nātak (M)*
dramatist	नाटककार	*nātakkār (M & F)*
essay	निबंध	*nibandh (M)*
essayist	निबंधकार	*nibandhkār (M & F)*
folk art	लोककला	*lōk-kalā (F)*
instrument (musical)	वाद्य	*vādya (M)*
music	संगीत	*sangīt (M)*
musician	संगीतकार	*sangītkār (M & F)*
novel	उपन्यास	*upanyās (M)*
novelist	उपन्यासकार	*upanyāskār (M & F)*

poet	कवि	*kavi (M & F)*
poetry	कविता	*kavirā (F)*
singer	गायक, गायिका	*gāyak (M), gayikā (F)*
song	गाना, गीत	*gānā, gīt (M)*
song (folk)	लोकगीत	*lōkgīt (F)*
story (folk)	लोक कथा	*lōk-kathā (F)*
story	कहानी	*kahānī (F)*
storywriter	कहानीकार	*kahānīkār (M & F)*

Chapter 18

Sports and Games

game	खेल	*khel (M)*
sports	खेल	*khel (M)*
sportsman	खिलाड़ी	*khilārī (M & F)*
team	टीम	*tīm (F)*
group	दल	*dal (M)*
playground	खेल का मैदान	*khel-kā-maidān (M)*
to win	जीतना	*jītnā (V)*
to lose	हारना	*hārnā (V)*

Health and Illness

abdominal pain	पेट का दर्द	*pet-kā dard(M)*
chickenpox	मोतीहारा, छोटी माता	*motīhārā, chottī matā(M & F)*
cold	जुकाम	*zukām (M)*
cough	खांसी	*khansī(F)*
fever	बुखार	*bukhār (M)*
malaria	मलेरिया	*maleriā(M)*
typhoid	मयादी बुखार	*mayādi bukhār (M)*
smallpox	चेचक	*chēchak (F)*
measles	खसरा	*khasrā(M)*
pain	दर्द	*dard (M)*
swelling	सूजन	*sūjan (M)*
medicine	दवा	*davā(M)*
medical treatment	इलाज	*ilāj (M)*
nausea	जी मचलाना	*jī machlānā(V)*
headache	सिर का दर्द	*sir-kā dard (M)*
whooping cough	काली खांसी	*kālī khānsī(F)*
dysentry	पेचिश	*pechish (F)*

Chapter 19
Relationship

relationship	रिश्ता	*rishtā (M)*
relative	रिश्तेदार	*rishtedār (M)*
father	पिता, बाप	*pitā, bāp (M)*
mother	माँ, माता	*mā, mātā (F)*
brother	भाई	*bhāi (M)*
sister	बहन	*bahin (F)*
husband	पति	*pati (M)*
wife	पत्नी	*patnī (F)*
son	बेटा	*betā, putrā (M)*
daughter	बेटी	*betī, putrī (F)*
nephew—		
(brother's son)	भतीजा	*bhatījā (M)*
(sister's son)	भतीजी	*bhatījī (M)*
niece—		
(brother's daughter)	भतीजा	*bhatījā (M)*
(sister's daughter)	भतीजा	*bhatījī (M)*
uncle—		
(father's brother)	चाचा	*chāchā (M0*
(his wife)	चाची	*chāchī (F)*

uncle—		
(mother's brother)	मामा	*māmā (M)*
(his wife)	मामी	*māmī (F)*

brother-in-law—		
(sister's husband)	बहनोई	*bahnoī (M)*
(wife's brother)	साला	*sālā (M)*

sister-in-law—		
(wife's sister)	साली	*sālī (F)*
(brother's wife)	भाभी	*bhābhī (F)*

father's sister	फूफी	*phūphī (F)*
(her husband)	फुफा	*phuphā (M)*
grandfather (paternal)	दादा	*dādā (M)*
grandmother (paternal)	दादी	*dādī (F)*
grandfather (maternal)	नाना	*nānā (M)*
grandmother (maternal)	नानी	*nānī (F)*
grandson (daughter's son)	पोता	*potā (M)*
granddaughter (daughter's daughter)	पोती	*potī (F)*

grandchildren	नाती, पोते	*nātī pote (M & F)*
family	परिवार	*parivār (M)*
son-in-law	दामाद	*dāmād (M)*
daughter-in-law	बहू	*bahū (F)*
step-mother	सौतेली माँ	*sautelī man (F)*
step-father	सौतेला बाप	*sautelā bāp (M)*

Chapter 20
Colours

black	काला	*kālā*
blue	नीला	*nīlā*
brown	भूरा	*bhurā*
green	हरा	*harā*
pink	गुलाबी	*gulabī*
yellow	पीला	*pīlā*
olive	मेहदी	*mehandī*
orange	नारंगी	*nārangī*
purple	बैंगनी	*baingnī*
white	सफेद	*safed*
bright	चमकीला	*chamkīlā*
gold	सुनहरा	*sunaharā*
rosy	गुलाबी	*gulābī*

Body Functions

chewing	चबाना	*chabana*
drinking	पीना	*pina*
eating	खाना	*khana*
hearing	सुनना	*sunana*
seeing	देखना	*dekhana*
smelling	सुंघना	*sunghana*

Sound of 'a' as in normal, formal; 'a' as in father, car; 'i' as in hit, sit; 'i' as in Delhi, machine; 'u' as in bull, full; 'u' as in crucible, crucial; e as in they, pet, red; 'ai' as in said; 'o' as in got, shot, so; 'o' as in moon, fool; 'au' as in audit, Paul.

Chapter 21
Everyday Vocabulary
दैनिक शब्दावली
Greetings

namaste	नमस्ते	*namastē*
namaskar	नमस्कार	*namaskār*
time	समय	*samay*
day	दिन	*din (M)*
morning	सवेरा	*saverā (M)*
afternoon	दोपहर	*dōpahar (M)*
evening	शाम	*shām (F)*
night	रात	*rāt (F)*
week	हफ्ता, सप्ताह	*haftā, saptah (M)*
fortnight	पखवाड़ा	*pakhwārā (M)*
month	महीना, मास	*mahinā, mās (M)*
year	साल, वर्ष	*sāl, varsh (M)*
decade	दशक	*dashak (M)*
century	सदी, शताब्दि	*sadī, shatābdi (F)*
today	आज	*aāj (M)*
yesterday	कल	*kal (M)*
tomorrow	कल	*kal (M)*
the day before yesterday	परसों	*parsōn (M)*
the day after	परसों	*parsōn (M)*

Numbers

one	एक	*ek*
two	दो	*dō*
three	तीन	*tīn*
four	चार	*chār*
five	पाँच	*pānch*
six	छ:	*chhah*
seven	सात	*sāt*
eight	आठ	*ath*
nine	नौ	*nāu*
ten	दस	*das*
eleven	ग्यारह	*gyārah*
twelve	बारह	*bārah*
thirteen	तेरह	*terah*
fourteen	चौदह	*chaudah*
fifteen	पन्द्रह	*pandrah*
sixteen	सोलह	*sōlah*
seventeen	सत्रह	*satrah*
eighteen	अठारह	*athārah*
nineteen	उन्नीस	*unnīs*
twenty	बीस	*bīs*

70

Ordinal Numbers

first	पहला	*pahlā*
second	दूसरा	*dusarā*
third	तीसरा	*tīsarā*
fourth	चौथा	*chauthā*
fifth	पाँचवां	*panchvān*
sixth	छठा	*chhathā*
seventh	सातवां	*sātavān*
eighth	आठवां	*athvān*
nineth	नौवां	*nāuvān*
tenth	दसवां	*dasavān*
eleventh	ग्यारहवां	*gyarahvan*
twelfth	बारहवां	*bārahvān*
thirteenth	तेरहवां	*terahvān*
fourteenth	चौदहवां	*chaudahvan*
fifteenth	पन्द्रहवां	*pandrahvān*
sixteenth	सोलहवां	*solahvān*

seventeenth	सत्रहवां	*satrahvān*
eighteenth	अठारहवां	*athārahvān*
nineteenth	उन्नीसवां	*unnīsvān*
twentieth	बीसवां	*bīsvān*
hundredth	सौवां	*sauvān*
thousandth	हज़ारवां	*hazāvān*
dozen	दर्जन	*darjan*
half a dozen	आधा दर्जन	*ahādarjan*

Planet

sun	सूर्य	*surya*
moon	चन्द्र	*chandra*
mars	मंगल	*mangal*
neptune	बुध	*budh*
jupiter	वृहस्पति	*brihaspati*
venus	शुक्र	*shukra*
saturn	शानि	*shāni*

Days of the Week

sunday	इतवार या रविवार	*itvār yā ravivār*
monday	सोमवार	*somvār*
tuesday	मंगलवार	*mangalvār*
wednesday	बुधवार	*budhvār*
thursday	बृहस्पतिवार	*brihaspativār*
friday	शुक्रवार	*shukravār*
saturday	शनिवार	*shanivār*

Directions

direction	दिशा	*dishā (F)*
east	पूर्व	*purva (M)*
west	पश्चिम	*pashchim (M)*
north	उत्तर	*uttar (M)*
south	दक्षिण	*dakshin (M)*

Sound of 'a' as in normal, formal; 'a' as in father, car, 'i' as in hit, sit; 'i' as in Delhi, machine; 'u' as in bull, full; 'u' as in crucible, crucial; e as in they, pet, red; 'ai' as in said; 'o' as in got, shot, sot; 'o' as in moon, fool; 'au' as in audit, Paul.

Chapter 22
Adjectives

angry	नाराज, गुस्सा	*nārāz, gussā*
annual	सालाना, वार्षिक	*sālānā, vārshik*
any	कोई	*koī*
bad	बुरा, खराब	*burā, khārab*
beautiful	सुन्दर	*sūndar*
better	बेहतर, ज्यादा अच्छा	*behtar, zyādā achchā*
big	बड़ा	*barā*
bitter	कडुवा	*karuvā*
blind	अन्धा	*andhā*
boiled	उबला हुआ	*ublāhuā*
bold	साहसी	*sāhasī*
brief	संक्षिप्त	*sankshipta*
broad	चौड़ा	*chaurā*
busy	व्यस्त, मसरूफ	*vyast, masruf*
calm	शान्त	*shānt*
capable	योग्य, लायक	*yogya, lāyak*
careless	लापरवाह	*lāparvāh*

central	बीच का	*bīch kā*
certain	विशिष्ट	*vishisht*
cheap	सस्ता	*sastā*
cheeful	खुश, प्रसन्न	*khush, prasanna*
clean	साफ	*sāf*
clear	साफ	*sāf*
clever	होशियार	*hōshiyār*
closed	बन्द	*band*
cold	ठन्डा	*thandā*
comfortable	आरामदेह	*arāmdeh*
common	आम	*ām*
cooked	पका हुआ	*pakā huā*
costly	महंगा	*mahangā*
courteous	विनायी	*vināyi*
cowardly	डरपोक	*darpōk*
damp	गीला	*gīlā*
dear (loved one)	प्यारा, प्रिय	*pyārā, priya*
decent	अच्छा	*achchā*
deep	गहरा	*gahrā*

dense	घना	*ghanā*
different	फर्क, भिन्न	*fark, bhinna*
difficult	कठिन, मुश्किल	*kathin, mūshkil*
dishonest	बेईमान	*beimān*
dirty	मैला, गन्दा	*mailā, gandā*
distant	दूर	*dur*
dry	सूखा	*sukhā*
dull (dim in intelligence)	बुद्धू	*buddhū*
dull (not quick)	सुस्त	*sūst*
dull (boring)	उबानेवाला	*ubanevālā*
dull (colourless)	फीका	*phīkā*
early	शुरू की	*shūru kī*
early (you are early)	आप जल्दी आ गये	*āp jaldī ā gaye*
early (give early reply)	जल्दी जवाब दीजिए	*jaldi jawāb dījiye*

easy	आसान, सरल	*āsān, saral*
economic	आर्थिक	*ārthik*
economic (frugal)	किफायतसार	*kifayātsār*
elder	बड़ा, उससे बड़ा	*barā usase barā*
empty	खाली	*khālī*
enough	काफी	*kāfī*
every	हर, प्रति	*har, prati*
fair (just)	उचित	*uchit*
fair (complexion)	गोरा	*gōrā*
fair (weather)	अच्छा, साफ	*achchhā, sāf*
faithful	वफादार	*vafādār*
false	झूठा	*jhuthā*
famous	मशहूर	*mashhūr*
fat	मोटा	*motā*
feeble	कमजोर	*kamzōr*
fertile	उपजाऊ	*upajaū*
fierce	भयंकर	*bhayankar*
happy	सुखी, खुश	*sukhī, khush*

hard	सख्त, कठोर	sakht, kathor
hasty	जल्दबाज	jalbhaz
healthy	स्वास्थ, तन्दुरूस्त	swasth, tandarust
heavy	भारी	bhari
high	ऊँचा	uncha
hollow	पोला	pola
holy	पवित्र	paavitra
honest	ईमानदार	imandar
hot	गरम	garam
humble	नम्र	namra
ignorant	अज्ञानी	agyani
ill	बीमार	bimar
imaginary	ख्याली, काल्पनिक	khyali, kalpanik
important	जरूरी	zaruri
innocent (naive)	नादान, भोला	nadan, bhola
innocent (of guilt)	निर्दोष, बेकसूर	nirdosh, bekasur
insane	पागल	pagal
interesting	दिलचस्प	dilchasp

jealous	ईर्ष्यालु	*irshyalū*
lame	लंगड़ा	*langrā*
large	बड़ा	*badā*
last	अन्तिम	*antim*
late (dead)	स्वर्गीय	*swargīya*
late (in time)	देर से	*der sē*
lazy	आलसी, सुस्त	*alāsi, sust*
lean	दुबला	*dublā*
learned	विद्वान	*vidvān*
light (weight)	हल्का	*halkā*
little (size)	छोटा	*chhūtā*
little (quantity)	थोड़ा कुछ	*thorā, kuchh*
long	लम्बा	*lambā*
low	नीचा	*nīchā*
mad	पागल	*pāgal*
many	बहुत	*bahut*
mean (person behaviour)	नीच	*nīch*
moral	नैतिक	*naitik*

much	बहुत	*bahut*
narrow	तंग, संकरा	*tag, sankrā*
national	राष्ट्रीय	*rashtrīya*
natural	कुदरती	*kudartī*
necessary	जरूरी	*zarurī*
next	दूसरा, अगला	*dusrā, aglā*
new	नया	*nayā*
notorious	बदनाम	*badnām*
obedient	आज्ञाकारी	*agyakārī*
official	सरकारी	*sarkari*
old (opp. of new)	पुराना	*purānā*
old (age)	बुड्ढा	*buddhā*
only	केवल, सिर्फ	*keval, sirf*
open	खुला	*khulā*
other	दूसरा	*dusarā*
patient	सब्रदार, धैर्यवान	*sabradār, dharyavān*
peaceful	शान्त	*shānt*
quiet	शान्त	*shānt*
rapid	तेज़	*tēz*

raw	कच्चा	*kachchā*
real	सच्चा	*sachchā*
religious	धार्मिक	*dhārmik*
respectful	सम्मानपूर्ण	*sammānpurna*
respected	सम्मानित	*sammānit*
rich	अमीर, धनी	*amīr, dhanī*
right (correct)	ठीक	*thik*
right (hand)	दाहिना, दायां	*dādinā, dāyaā*
ripe	पक्का	*pakkā*
rough (texture)	खुरदुरा	*khurdurā*
round	गोल	*gol*
rude	बदतमीज	*badtamīz*
rural	देहाती	*dehātī*
sacred	पवित्र	*pavitra*
sad	उदास, दुखी	*udās, dukhī*
safe	सुरक्षित	*surakshit*
same	वही, वैसा ही	*vahī, vaisāhī*
secret	गुप्त, रहस्य	*gupt, rahasya*
severe	सख्त, कठोर	*sakht, kathōr*

shallow	छिछला	*chhichlā*
sharp	तेज़	*tēz*
short (brief)	छोटा	*chhōtā*
short (stature)	नाटा	*nātā*
silken	रेशमी	*rēshamī*
slow (speed)	धीरे	*dhīre*
slow (backward, not smart)	पीछे, सुस्त	*pīchhē, sust*
small	छोटा	*chhōtā*
social	सामाजिक	*sāmājik*
soft	नरैम, मुलायम	*naram, mulāyam*
solid	ठोस	*thōs*
some	कुछ	*kūchh*
sour	खट्टा	*khattā*
special	खास	*khās*
stale	बासी	*bāsī*
strange	विचित्र, अजीब	*vichitra, ajīb*
strong	मजबूत	*mazbūt*
stupid	बेवकूफ, मूर्ख	*bēvakuf, mūrkh*

83

successful	सफल	*saphal*
such	ऐसा	*aisā*
sure	निश्चित	*nishchit*
sweet	मीठा	*mīṭhā*
swift	तेज़	*tēz*
tasty	स्वादिष्ट	*svādisht*
tender	नरम, मुलायम	*naram, mulāyam*
thick	मोटा	*mōṭā*
thin (person, annual)	दुबला	*dublā*
thin (neuter gender)	पतला	*patlā*
thirsty	प्यासा	*pyāsā*
tight	तंग, कसा	*tang, kasā*
tired	थका	*thakā*
true	सच	*sach*
ugly	बदसूरत	*badsurat*
vain	घमंडी	*ghamandī*
weak	कमजोर	*kamzōr*
wily	चालाक	*chālāk*
wise	बुद्धिमान	*buddhiman*
zealous	उत्साही	*utsāhī*

Bodily defects

bald	गंजा	*ganjā*
blind	अन्धा	*andhā*
deaf	बहरा	*baharā*
dumb	गूंगा	*gungā*
lame	लंगड़ा	*langarā*
one-eyed	काना	*kānā*

Sound of 'a' as in normal, formal; 'a' as in father, car, 'i' as in hit, sit; 'i' as in Delhi, machine; 'u' as in bull, full; 'u' as in crucible, crucial; e as in they, pet, red; 'ai' as in said; 'o' as in got, shot, so; 'o' as in moon, fool; 'au' as in audit, Paul.

Verb Chart

Infinitive		Present Indefinite	Present Continuous	Present Perfect	Past Indefinite	Past Continuous	Past Perfect	Future
जाना jānā	I s*	(मैं) jātā hūṅ (main) jātā hūṅ	जा रहा हूँ jā rahā hūṅ	गया हूँ gayā hūṅ	जाता था jātā thā	जा रहा था jā rahā thā	गया था gayā thā	जाऊँगा jāūṅgā
	p**	(हम) jāte hain	जा रहे हैं jā rahe hain	गये हैं gaye hain	जाते थे jāte the	जा रहे थे jā rahe the	गये थे gaye the	जायेंगे jāyeṅge
	II s	(तुम) jāte ho	जा रहे हो jā rahe ho	गये हो gaye ho	जाते थे jāte the	जा रहे थे jā rahe the	गये थे gaye the	जाओगे jāoge
	p	(आप) jāte hain (आप लोग) jāte hain	जा रहे हैं jā rahe hain	गये हैं gaye hain	जाते थे jāte the	जा रहे थे jā rahe the	गये थे gaye the	जाओगे jāoge
	III s	(वह) जाता है jātā hain	जा रहा है* jā rahā hai	गया है gayā hai	जाता था jātā thā	जा रहा था jā rahā thā	गया था gayā thā	जायेगा jāyegā
	p	(वे) jāte hain	जा रहे हैं jā rahe hain	गये हैं gaye hain	जाते थे jāte the	जा रहे थे jā rahe the	गये थे gaye the	जायेंगे jāyeṅge
आना ānā	I s	(मैं) आता हूँ ātā hūṅ	आ रहा हूँ ā rahā hūṅ	आया हूँ āyā hūṅ	आता था ātā thā	आ रहा था ā rahā thā	आया था āyā thā	आऊँगा āūṅgā
	p	(हम) आते हैं āte hain	आ रहे हैं ā rahe hain	आये हैं āye hain	आते थे āte the	आ रहे थे ā rahe the	आये थे āye the	आयेंगे āyeṅge
	II s	(तुम) आते हो āte ho	आ रहे हो ā rahe ho	आये हो āye ho	आते थे āte the	आ रहे थे ā rahe the	आये थे āye the	आओगे āoge
	p	(आप) āte hain (आप लोग) āte hain	आ रहे हैं ā rahe hain	आये हैं āye hain	आते थे āte the	आ रहे थे ā rahe the	आये थे āye the	आओगे āoge
	III s	(वह) आता है ātā hai	आ रहा है ā rahā hai	आया है āyā hai	आता था ātā thā	आ रहा था ā rahā thā	आया था āyā thā	आयेगा āyegā
	p	(वे) āte hain	आ रहे हैं ā rahe hain	आये हैं āye hain	आते थे āte the	आ रहे थे ā rahe the	आये थे āye the	आयेंगे āyeṅge

Chapter 23

Verbs

to accept	स्वीकार करना	*savīkār karnā*
to admire	प्रशंसा करना	*prashansā karnā*
to advise	सलाह देना	*salāh denā*
to answer	जवाब देना	*javāb denā*
to argue	बहस देना	*bahas karnā*
to arrange	इन्तजाम करना	*intazām karnā*
to arrive	पहुंचना	*pahunchnā*
to arrest	गिरफ्तार करना	*giraftār karnā*
to ask	पूछना	*puchhnā*
to attack	हमला करना	*hamlā karnā*
to attempt	कोशिश करना	*kōshish karnā*
to awake	जागना	*jāganā*
to be	होना	*hōnā*
to be afraid	डरना	*darnā*
to be angry	नाराज होना	*nārāz hōnā*
to be tired	थका होना	*thakā hōnā*
to bathe	नहाना	*nahānā*
to bear (tolerate	सहना	*sahnā*

to bear the burden	भार उठाना	*bhār uthānā*
to become	होना, हो जाना	*honā, hō jānā*
to beat	मारना, पीटना	*mārnā, pītnā*
to beat (egg)	फैंटना	*phentnā*
to beg	भीख मागंना	*bhīkh māngnā*
to begin	शुरू करना	*shuru karnā*
to believe	विश्वास करना	*vishvās karnā*
to bite	काटना	*kātnā*
to blame	दोष देना	*dōsh denā*
to boil (tr.)	उबालना	*ubālnā*
to boil (int.)	उबालना	*ubālnā*
to break (tr.)	तोड़ना	*tōrnā*
to break (int.)	टूटना	*tūtna*
to breath	सांस लेना	*sāns lenā*
to bring	लाना	*lānā*
to build	बनाना	*banānā*
to burn (tr.)	जलना	*jalnā*
to burn (int.)	जलाना	*jalānā*
to burst	फाड़ना	*phārnā*
to burst (int.)	फूटना	*phūtnā*

to buy	खरीदना	*kharīdnā*
to call	बुलाना	*bulānā*
to care	परवाह करना	*parvāh karnā*
to carry	उठाना	*uthānā*
to catch	पकड़ना	*pakarnā*
to change	बदलना	*badalnā*
to change (int.)	बदल जाना	*badal janā*
to chop	छोटे टुकडे काटना	*chhōtē tukrē kātnā*
to clean	साफ करना	*sāf karnā*
to climb	चढ़ना	*charhnā*
to desire	चाहना	*chāhnā*
to die	मरना	*marnā*
to dig	खोदना	*khōdnā*
to dine	खाना	*khānā*
to do	करना	*karnā*
to doubt	शक करना	*shak karnā*
to draw	खीचना	*khīmchnā*
to dream	सपना देखना	*sapnā dekhnā*
to dress	कपड़े पहिनना	*kapre pahin-nā*

to drink	पीना	*pīnā*
to drive (a car)	मोटर चलाना	*mōtar chalnā*
to dry (tr.)	सुखाना	*sukhānā*
to dry (int..)	सुखना	*sukhanā*
to eat	खाना	*khānā*
to exclaim	चिल्लाना	*chillānā*
to explain	समझाना	*samjhānā*
to excuse	माफ करना	*māf karnā*
to examine	परीक्षा करना	*parīkshā karnā*
to fall	गिरना	*girnā*
to fear	डरना	*darnā*
to feed	खिलाना	*khilānā*
to feel	अनुभव करना	*anubhav karnā*
to fight	लड़ना	*larnā*
to fill	भरना	*bharnā*
to find	पाना	*pānā*
to finish	खत्म करना	*khatm karnā*
to forget	भूलना	*bhulnā*
to forgive	माफ करना	*māf karnā*
to freeze	जमाना	*jamānā*

to freeze (int.)	जमना	*jamnā*
to fry	तलना	*talnā*
to get	पाना	*pānā*
to get up	उठना	*uthnā*
to give	देना	*denā*
to give up	छोड़ देना	*chhoṝ denā*
to go	जाना	*jānā*
to go in	अन्दर जाना	*andar jānā*
to go out	बाहर जाना	*bāhar jānā*
to get out	बाहर निकलना	*bāhar nikalnā*
to grind	पीसना	*pīsnā*
to grow	बढ़ना	*barhnā*
to guide	रास्ता दिखाना	*rāstā dikānā*
to increase	बढ़ना	*barhnā*
to insult	अपमान करना	*apmān karnā*
to irrigate	सिंचना	*sichnā*
to irritate	नाराज करना	*nārāz karnā*
to introduce	परिचय कराना	*parichay karānā*
to joke	मजाक करना	*mazāk karnā*
to jump	कूदना	*kudanā*

to keep	रखना	*rakhnā*
to kick	लात मारना	*lāt mārnā*
to kill	जान से मारना	*jān sē mārnā*
to kiss	चूमना	*chmnā*
to know	जानना	*jānanā*
to laugh	हंसना	*hansnā*
to lay the table	मेज लगाना	*mēz lagānā*
to lead (the way)	रास्ता दिखाना	*rāstā dikhānā*
to learn	सीखना	*sīkhnā*
to lend	उधार देना	*udhār denā*
to lie down	लेटना	*lātnā*
to lie (telling)	झूठ बोलना	*jhūth boonā*
to lift	उठाना	*uthānā*
to like	पसन्द करना	*pasand karnā*
to look	देखना	*dekhnā*
to lose	खोना	*khōnā*
to love	प्यार करना	*pyār karnā*
to make	बनाना	*banānā*
to marry	शादी करना	*shādī karnā*
to measure	नापना	*nāpanā*

to meet	मिलना	*milnā*
to memorize	रटना	*ratnā*
to move	सरकाना	*sarkāna*
to move (int.)	सरकना	*sarkanā*
to move on	आगे सरकाना	*age sarkānā*
to obey	कहना मानना,	*kohnā manānā*
	आज्ञा मानना	*agyā mānanā*
to object	आपत्ति करना	*apatti karnā*
to offend	नाराज करना	*nārāz karnā*
to open	खोलना	*kholnā*
to open (int.)	खुलना	*khulnā*
to order	आज्ञा देना	*agyā denā*
to paint (to colour)	रंगना, रंग करना	*rangnā, rang karnā*
to paint a picture	चित्र बनाना	*chitra banānā*
to raise	उठाना	*uthānā*
to read	पढ़ना	*parhnā*
to receive	पाना	*pānā*
to recommend	सिफारिश करना	*sifārish kairnā*
to refuse	मना करना	*manā karnā*

93

to regret	अफसोस करना	*afsos karnā*
to reject	अस्वीकार करना	*asvikār karnā*
to remember	याद करना	*yād karnā*
to rest	आराम करना	*ārām karnā*
to return	लौटाना	*lautānā*
to return (int.)	लौटना	*lautanā*
to ring (the bell)	घन्टी बजाना	*ghantī bajānā*
to ride	सवार होना	*savār honā*
to rinse	ढोना	*dhonā*
to roast	भूनना	*bhunanā*
to run	दौड़ना	*daurnā*
to run away	भाग जाना	*bhāg jānā*
to say	कहना	*kahnā*
to scold	डांटना	*dāntnā*
to search	ढूंढना	*dhundhanā*
to see	देखना	*dekhnā*
to sell	बेचना	*bechnā*
to send	भेजना	*bhejnā*
to send for	बुला भेजना	*bulā bhejnā*
to serve	सेवा करना	*sevā karnā*

to sew	सीना	$s\overline{m}\overline{a}$
to shake	हिलाना	$hil\overline{a}n\overline{a}$
to shake (int.)	हिलना	$hiln\overline{a}$
to shake hands	हाथ मिलाना	$h\overline{a}th\ mil\overline{a}n\overline{a}$
to shave	दाढ़ी बनाना	$d\overline{a}rh\overline{i}\ ban\overline{a}n\overline{a}$
to shout	चिल्लाना	$chill\overline{a}n\overline{a}$
to show	दिखाना	$dikh\overline{a}n\overline{a}$
to sing	गाना	$g\overline{a}n\overline{a}$
to sink	डूबना	$duban\overline{a}$
to sit	बैठना	$baithan\overline{a}$
to sleep	सोना	$s\overline{o}n\overline{a}$
to (put to) sleep	सुलाना	$sul\overline{a}n\overline{a}$
to smell	सूंघना	$sunghn\overline{a}$
to smile	मुस्कराना	$muskar\overline{a}n\overline{a}$
to sneeze	छींकना	$chh\overline{i}mkn\overline{a}$
to sow	बोना	$b\overline{o}n\overline{a}$
to speak	बोलना	$b\overline{o}ln\overline{a}$
to spit	थूकना	$thukn\overline{a}$
to stand	खड़ा होना	$khar\overline{a}\ h\overline{o}n\overline{a}$
to stay	ठहरना	$thaharn\overline{a}$

to steal	चुराना	*churanā*
to stop	रूकना	*rukhā*
to strike	मारना	*mārnā*
to strike (work)	हड़ताल करना	*hartāl karnā*
to study	पढ़ना	*parhnā*
to suspect	शक करना	*shak karnā*
to swear	कसम खाना	*kasam khanā*
to abuse	गाली देना	*gālī denā*
to swim	तैरना	*tairnā*
to take	लेना	*lenā*
to taste	चखना	*chakhnā*
to tear	फाड़ना	*phārnā*
to tell	बताना	*batānā*
to think	सोचना	*sōchanā*
to try	कोशिश करना	*kōshish karnā*
to thank	धन्यवाद देना	*dhanyavād denā*
to throw	फैंकना	*phainknā*
to tighten	कसना	*kasnā*
to translate	अनुवाद करना	*anuvād karnā*
to understand	समझना	*samajhanā*

to undress	कपड़े उतारना	*kapre utārnā*
to use	उपयोग करना	*upayog karnā*
to utter	कहना	*kahnā*
to walk	चलना	*chalnā*
to walk for pleasure	सैर करना	*sair karnā*
to want	चाहना	*chāhnā*
to wash	धोना	*dhonā*
to waste	बरबाद करना	*barbād karnā*
to water (the plants)	पानी देना	*pānī denā*
to wear	पहनना	*pahannā*
to weave	बुनना	*bunanā*
to weep	रोना	*ronā*
to weigh	तोलना	*tolnā*
to whistle	सीटी बजाना	*sītī bajānā*
to wish	चाहना	*chāhnā*
to win	जीतना	*jītanā*
to work	काम करना	*kām karnaā*
to write	लिखना	*likhnā*
to yell	चिल्लाना	*chillānā*

Some other useful words and phrases

to finish (int.)	खत्म होना	*khatam hōnā*
to finish (tr.)	खत्म करना	*khatam karnā*
specially, particularly	खास कर	*khās kar*
please excuse me	क्षमा कीजिए	*kshāma kījiye*
sorry, I am late	अफसोस है, देर हो गई	*afsos hai, der ho gayī*
I am early	मैं जल्दी आ गया।	*main jaldi ā gayā*
does not matter	कोई बात नहीं	*koī bāt nahin*
please don't mind	बुरा न मानिये	*burā na maniye*
please	कृपया, कृपा करके	*kripayā, kripa karkē*
to put on shoes	जूता पहनना	*jutā pahnanā*
to celebrate	खुशी मनाना, उत्सव मनाना	*khushi manānā, utsava manānā*
to congratulate	बधाई देना, मुबारकबाद देना	*badhāī denā mubarakbād dena*
congratulations	बधाई	*badhāī*
happy new year	नया साल मुबारक हो।	*nayā sāl mubārak hō*

best wishes for the new year	नये वर्ष की शुभकामनाएं।	*naye̅ varsh ki̅ shubhakamana̅en*
good wishes for birthday	जन्मदिन मुबारक हो।	*janmadin muba̅rak ho̅*
good wishes	शुभकामनाएँ।	*shubhaka̅mana̅en*

Various uses of the word tez

The fever is high.	बुखार तेज है।	bukhār tēz hai.
The sun is strong.	धूप तेज है।	dhip tēz hai.
The knife is sharp.	छूरी तेज है।	chhurē tēz hai.
The boy is sharp (int.)	लड़का तेज है।	larkā tēz hai.
The light is strong.	रोशनी तेज है।	roshanī tēz hai.
The wind is strong.	हवा तेज है।	havā tēz hai.
He runs fast.	वह तेज दौड़ता है।	vah tēz daratā hai.
Take tea after take the medicine.	दवा खाकर चाय पीजिए।	davā khākar chāy pījiye
Sleep after eating.	खाना खाकर सो जाइए।	khānā khākar so jāiye.
I shall go for a walk after dinner.	मैं खाना खाकर घूमने जाऊँगा।	main khānā khakar ghūmane jāungā.
After reading tell me how the book is.	पढ़कर बताइए। ये किताब कैसी है?	parh karbatāiye ye kitāb kaisī hai?

Chapter 24

Cooking term

to bake	सेंकना	*senkanā*
to boil	उबालना	*ubālnā*
to chill	ठन्डा करना	*thandā karnā*
to chop	छोटे टुकड़े करना	*chhote tukre karnā*
to cut	काटना	*kātanā*
to cover	ढकना	*dhakanā*
to dice	टुकड़े करना	*tukrē karanā*
to fry	तलना	*talnā*
to grate	कसना	*kasnā*
to grind	पीसना	*pīsanā*
to freeze	जमना	*jamanā*
to mash	मसलना	*masalnā*
to peel	छीलना	*chhīlnā*
to scrape	खुरचना	*khurachanaā*
spices	मसाले	*masāle*
to strain	छानना	*chānanā*
to season	तड़का देना	*tadkā denā*
to warm up	गरम करना	*garam karnā*
to wash	धोना	*dhonā*

The Wallah

Some foreigners living in India have adopted the word 'wallah' to mean a hawker. Actually the word spelt phonetically is **vala,** and by itself it does not have any meaning, but when combined with other words it has a variety of meanings. For example, when combined with the name of a commodity it would mean the seller of that particular commodity, e.g.,

सब्जीवाला	vegetable vendor	*Sabjivālā*
फलवाला	fruit vendor	*Phalvālā*
फूलवाला	flower vendor	*Phulvālā*
कपड़े वाला	cloth vendor	*Kapravālā*
बरतन वाला	utensils vendor	*Bartanvālā*
अखबार वाला	newspaperman	*Akhbarvālā*
दूध वाला	milkman	*Dudhvālā*
खिलोने वाला	toy-seller	*Khilōnevālā*
टैक्सी वाला	taxi-driver	*Taxīvālā*

But that is not all. **Vala** may be combined with name of a city or town to mean a person belonging to that place, e.g., **Dillivala, Bombayvala,** and so on.

Vala is also used to specify a certain thing. For example **kalvala akhbar,** means yesterday's newspaper; **uparvala kamara** means the room upstairs.

The meaning would be the same if you same kal ka Akhbar or upar ka kamara, but vala is idiomatic and a colloquial expression.

Sound of 'a' as in normal, formal; 'a' as in father, car; 'i' as in hit, sit; 'i' as in Delhi, machine, 'u' as in bull, full; 'u' as in crucible, crucial; e as in they, pet, red, 'ai' as in said; 'o' as in got, shot, so; 'o' as in moon, fool; ''au' as in audit, Paul.

PART III

PHRASES AND SENTENCES

A large number of readers do not want to perfect their study of a language but prefer to acquire colloquial practice. For the benefit of such people we are, hereafter, giving short sentences for practically all occasions. To those who want to avoid the study of grammar, these ready made sentences like the ready made clothes would come in handy. And even for those who prefer to study the grammar, these sentences would provide very useful steps.

In this part we have given 695 phrases and sentences. Natrually all can not be equally important. Readers are, therefore requested to learn small phrases in the first instance.

Once they have mastered the phrases, they should concentrate on short sentences. The longer sentences should be taken up only at the end. We trust tha a study of only this part will enbable readers to express themselves in Hindi.

Sound of 'a' as in normal, formal; 'a' as in father, car; 'i' as in hit, sit 'i' as in Delhi, machine, 'u' as in bull, full; 'u' as in crucible, crucial; e as in they, pet, red; 'ai' as in said; 'o' as in got, shot, so;l 'o' as in moon, fool; 'au' as in audit, Paul.

Chapter 25
Useful Words and Expressions

1.	I	मैं	1. *Main*
2.	We	हम	2. *ham*
3.	You	आप	3. *Ap*
4.	She	वह	4. *Vah*
5.	He	वह	5. *Vah*
6.	They	वे	6. *Ve*
7.	My	मेरा (m);	7. *Merā(m);*
		मेरी (f)	*Merī(f)*
8.	Not Mine	मेरा नहीं (m);	8. *Merā Nabhīm (m);*
		मेरी नहीं (f)	*Merī Nabhīm (f)*
9.	Yours	आपका	9. *Apkā*

10.	Not yours	आपका नहीं	*Apka Nahīn*
11.	His	उनका	*Unkā*
12.	Her	उनका	*Unkā*
13.	Our	हमारा	*Hamārā*
14.	Their	उनका	*Unkā*
15.	To me	मुझको	*Mujhakō*
16.	To her	उनको	*Unkō*
17.	To them	उनको	*Unkō*
18.	Yes	हाँ	*Han*
19.	No	नहीं	*Nahīn*
20.	Please	कृपया	*Kripayā*
21.	Good	अच्छा	*Achchhā*
22.	Not Good	अच्छा नहीं	*Achchhā Nahīn*

23.	Bad	खराब	*Kharāb*
24.	Perhaps	शायद	*Shāyad*
25.	Nothing	कुछ नहीं	*Kuchh nahīṁ*
26.	Thanks	धन्यवाद	*Dhanyavād*
27.	Thank you	आपको बहुत धन्यवाद	*Apko bahut dhanyavād*
28.	Downstairs	नीचे	*Nīche*
29.	Upstairs	ऊपर	*Upar*
30.	Straight	सीधे	*Sīdhe*
31.	Back	पीछे	*Pīchhe*
32.	To the right	दाहिनी तरफ	*Dāhinī taraf*
33.	To the left	बायीं तरफ	*Bāēṁ taraf*
34.	On the other side	दूसरी तरफ	*Dusarī taraf*

35.	Now	अब	*Ab*
36.	Soon	जल्दी	*Jaldī*
37.	Why?	क्यों ?	*Kyon?*
38.	When?	कब ?	*Kab?*
39.	How?	कैसे ?	*Kaise?*
40.	Who?	कौन ?	*Kaun?*
41.	Whom?	कौन को ?	*Kaun ko?*
42.	Whose?	किसका ?	*Kishkā?*
43.	Because	क्योंकि	*Kyonki*
44.	Look	देखिए	*Dekhiya*
45.	Listen	सुनिए	*Suniye*
46.	Come in	अन्दर आइये	*Andar āiye*

47.	Take care	ध्यान रखिये	*Dhyān rakhiye*
48.	More haste	जल्दी कीजिए	*Jaldī Kījiye*
49.	Come along	साथ चले आइये	*Sāth chale āiye*
50.	Much	अधिक	*Adhik*
51.	Little	थोड़ा	*Thorā*
52.	Enough	काफी	*Kāfi*
53.	All	सब	*Sab*
54.	Where	कहाँ	*Kahān*
55.	Here	यहाँ	*Yahān*
56.	There	वहाँ	*Vahān*
57.	Here	इस तरफ	*Is taraf*
58.	There	उस तरफ	*Us taraf*
59.	Far	दूर	*Dur*

60.	near	पास	*Pas*
61.	Inside	भीतर	*Bhītar*
62.	Outside	बाहर	*Bāhar*
63.	Walk in	अन्दर चलिए	*Andar chaliye*
64.	This way	इस रास्ते से	*Is rāste se*
65.	That way	उस रास्ते से	*Us rāste se*
66.	Not this way	इस रास्ते से नहीं	*Is rāste se nahīṅ*
67.	Not that way	उस रास्ते से नहीं	*Us rāste se nahīṅ*
68.	In this way	इस तरह	*Is tarah*
69.	Too soon	बहुत जल्दी	*Bahut jaldī*
70.	Too late	बहुत देर	*Bahut der*
71.	Soon or later	जल्दी या देर से	*Jaldīyāder se*
72.	Very well	बहुत अच्छा	*Bahut achchhā*

110

73.	Not very well	बहुत अच्छा नहीं	*Bahut achchhā nahīṁ*
74.	Carry this	इसको ले चलिए	*Iskō le chaliye*
75.	Put this	इसको रखिए	*Isko rakhiye*
76.	Bring me	मुझको लाइये	*Mujhko lāye*
77.	Give me	मुझको दीजिए	*Mujhko dījiya*
78.	Send me	मुझको भेजिए	*Mujhko bhejiye*
79.	Take this way	इसको ले जाइये	*Isko le jāye*
80.	Please accept	कृपया स्वीकार कीजिए	*Krpayā̃ savīkār kījiye*
81.	...Help...	...सहायता कीजिये	*... Sahāā kījiye*
82.	...Give...	...दीजिए	*...Dījiye*
83.	...Take...	...लीजिए	*...Lījiye*
84.	...Sit down...	...बैठ जाइए	*...Baith jāye*

111

85.	...Smoke (Cigarette)...	...सिगरेट पीजिए	...*Cigarette pījiye*
86.	...Write this...	...यह लिखिये	...*Yah likhiye*
87.	...Tell him...	...उनसे कहिये	.....*Unse kahiye*
88.	...Show...	...दिखाइये	...*Dikhāiye*
89.	I know	मैं जानता हूं	*Main jāntā hūn*
90.	Change the water daily.	रोज पानी बदलो	*Roy pānī badlo*
91.	Take this rubbish away.	यह कचरा ले जाओ।	*Yah kachrā le jāo*
92.	What does it resemble?	यह किस जैसा है?	*Yah kis jaisā hai?*
93.	I shall fine you.	मैं आपको दण्ड दूंगा	*Main āpko dand dūngā*
94.	Let him go out.	उसको बाहर जाने दो	*Usko bāhar jāne do*
95.	Let him come in.	उसको अन्दर आने दो।	*Usko andar āne do*

112

96.	Do it today instead of tomorrow	कल के बदले आज करो।	Kal ke badle aaj karo tomorrow.
97.	Where does Mr. Ravi live?	रवि साहब कहां रहते हैं?	Ravi sāhab kahān rahate hain?
98.	This book is good.	यह किताब अच्छी है।	Yah kitāb achchā hai
99.	Where are you going?	आप कहां जा रहे हैं?	Āp kahān jā rahe hain?
100.	How do you do?	कहिए क्या हाल है?	Kahiye kyā hāl hai?
101.	When shall I come?	मैं कब आऊं?	Main kab ātūn?
102.	I cannot speak Hindustani.	मैं हिन्दुस्तानी नहीं बोल सकता हूं।	Main Hindustānī nahin bol sakatā hun.
103.	Hurry up.	जल्दी कीजिये।	Jalī Kījiye
104.	Come along.	साथ-साथ आइये।	Sāth sāth āiye
105.	This way	इस तरफ से	Is taraf se

113

106.	That way	उस तरफ से	Us taraf se
107.	Not this way	इस तरफ से नहीं	Is taraf se nahīṁ
108.	Sooner or later	जल्दी या देर से	Jaldī yā der se
109.	Never mind	परवाह नहीं	Parwāh nahīṁ
110.	Do you know?	क्या आप जानते हैं?	Kyā āp jānte hain?
111.	Do you understand?	क्या आप समझते हैं?	Kyā āp samajhate hain?
112.	How much time?	कितनी देर लगेगी?	Kitnī der lagegī?
113.	When do we reach?	हम कब तक पहुंचेगे?	Ham kab tak pahunchenge?
114.	Where have you come from?	आप कहाँ से आये है?	Āp kahān se āye hain?
115.	What for?	किस लिए?	Kis liye

114

116.	How do you know?	आपको कैसे मालूम है?	Āpko kaise malum hai?
117.	I am in a hurry.	मैं जल्दी में हूं।	Main jaldi mein hun.
118.	Do you smoke?	क्या आप धूम्रपान करते हैं?	Kyā āp dumarpan karte?
119.	On which floor?	किस मंजिल पर है।	Kis manjil par hain
120.	Without doubt.	बिना शक, निस्संदेह।	Bina shak, Nisandeh
121.	All at once	यकायक	Yak āyak
122.	It is not my fault.	यह मेरा दोष नहीं है।	Yah merā dosh nahīn hai
123.	Is there a phone (call for me)?	क्या मेरा फोन आया है?	Kyā merā pbon āyā hai?
124.	Good morning	नमस्कार – नमस्ते	Namaskār- Namastey

115

125.	Good day	नमस्कार – नमस्ते	125.	*Namaskār-Namastey*
126.	Good evening	नमस्कार – नमस्ते	126.	*Namaskār-Namastey*
127.	Good night	नमस्कार – विदा	127.	*Nāmaskar-vidā*
128.	Good bye	नमस्कार – नमस्ते	128.	*Namaskār-Namastey*
129.	Do you not understand?	क्या आप नहीं समझते?	129.	*Kyā āp nahīm samjhate?*
130.	What do you want?	आपको क्या चाहिये ?	130.	*Āpko kyā chāhiye?*
131.	I do not want.	मुझे नहीं चाहिये।	131.	*Mujhe nahīm chāhiye*
132.	Leave me alone.	मुझे अकेले छोड़ दीजिये।	132.	*Mujhe akele chhor dij̄iye*
133.	Have we got time?	क्या हमारे पास समय है?	133.	*Kyā hamāre pās samay hai?*

116

134.	How much time will it take?	इसमें कितना समय लगेगा?	*Is men kitanā samay lagegā*
135.	When do we start?	हम कब रवाना होंगे?	*Ham kab ravānā honge?*
136.	When do we reach?	हम कब पहुंचेंगे?	*Ham kab pahunchenge?*
137.	Where do we meet?	हम लोग कहाँ मिलेंगे?	*Ham lōg kahan milengē?*
138.	Who will take us there?	हमको वहाँ कौन ले जावेगा?	*Hamko vahān kaun le jāvegā*
139.	Do not go away.	चले न जाइये।	*Chale na jāi-ye*
140.	How are you?	आप कैसे हैं?	*Āp kaise hain?*
141.	How do you do?	आप कैसे हैं?	*Āp kaise hain?*
142.	Glad to meet you.	आपसे मिल कर खुशी हुई।	*Āp se mil kar khūshī huī*

117

143.	With pleasure.	ख़ुशी से।	*Khushi se*
144.	Yes Sir,	जी हाँ	*Jī hān*
145.	Give my compliments to	मेरा नमस्कार	*Merā namaskār*
146.	Pay my regards to	मेरा नमस्कार	*Merā Namaskār*
147.	I am obliged.	मैं आभारी हूं	*Main abhārī hun*
148.	This is my duty.	यह मेरा फ़र्ज़ है।	*Yah merā faras hai*
149.	Beg your pardon	क्षमा कीजिए।	*Kshamā kījiye*
150.	Excuse me.	क्षमा कीजिए।	*Kshamā kījiye*
151.	I am sorry.	मुझे अफ़सोस है।	*Mujhe afsos hai*
152.	I am mistaken.	मुझ से भूल हुई।	*Mujh se bhul bui*
153.	What do you want?	आप क्या चाहते हैं?	*Ap kya chahate hain?*
154.	May I see you?	क्या मैं आपसे मिल सकता हूँ?	*Kyā main āpse mil saktā hun?*

155.	Please explain.	कृपया समझा दीजिये।	*Kripayā samajbā dījiye*
156.	I have no objection.	मुझे कोई एतराज़ नहीं है।	*Mujhe koī etrāj nahīn hai*
157.	It is true.	यह सत्य है।	*Yah satya hai*
158.	With pleasure	बड़ी खुशी से	*Barī khushī se*
159.	As you with.	जैसी आपकी इच्छा	*Jaisī āpskī icbchā*
160.	Not so costly.	इतना महंगा नहीं है।	*Itnā mehngā nahīn hai*
161.	Happy New Year.	नव वर्ष शुभ हो।	*Nav varsh shubb ho*
162.	Congratulations.	बधाई।	*Vadhāī*
163.	Excellent.	बहुत सुन्दर	*Bahut sundar*
164.	What?	क्या?	*Kyā?*

165.	Where have you come from?	आप कहाँ से आये हैं?	Āp kahān se āye hain?
166.	What for?	किस लिये?	Kis liye?
167.	Where to?	कहाँ को?	Kahān ko?
168.	Who has sent you?	आपको किसने भेजा है?	Āpko kisane bhejā hai?
169.	How do you know?	आप कैसे जानते हैं?	Āp kaise jānate hai?
170.	I am in a hurry.	मैं जल्दी में हूँ।	Main jaldī men hun
171.	I am late.	मुझे देर हो गई।	Mujhe der bo gaī
172.	On whcih floor?	किस मंजिल पर?	Kis manzil par?
173.	On the first floor.	पहली मंजिल पर।	Pahalī manzio par
174.	—second floor	दूसरी—	Dusarī

175.	—third floor.	तीसरी—	*Tīsarī*
176.	—fourth floor.	चौथी—	*Chauthī*
177.	–fifth floor.	पाँचवीं—	*Panchavī*
178.	—sixth floor	छठी—	*Chhaṭhī*
179.	—seventh floor.	सातवीं—	*Sātavī*
180.	From top to bottom.	ऊपर से नीचे तक।	*Uper se nīche tak*
181.	I am going out.	मैं (f) बाहर जा रही हूँ।	*Main (f) bāhar jā rahī hun*
182.	I shall not come till noon.	मैं (m) दोपहर तक नहीं आऊंगा	*Main (m) dophar tak nahīn aūngā*
183.	—afternoon.	— तीसरे पहर —	—*tīsara pahar*—
184.	—evening	— शाम —	—*shām*—
185.	—night.	— रात —	—*rāt*—

121

186.	Are you going anywhere?	क्या आप (m) कहीं बाहर जा रहे हैं?	Kyā āp (m) kahin bāhar jā rahe hain?
187.	For want of time.	समय न होने से	Samay na hone se
188.	That depends on you.	यह आप पर निर्भर है।	Yah āp par nirbhar hai
189.	Without a doubt.	बिना शक।	Binā shak
190.	You (m) are joking.	आप (m) मजाक कर रहे हैं।	Āp mazāk kar rahe hain
191.	I (m) am not joking.	मैं (m) मजाक नहीं कर रहा हूं।	Main mazāk nahīn kar rahā hun
192.	All at once.	सब एक साथ।	Sab ek sāth
193.	I (m) recognize.	मैं (m) पहचानता हूँ	Main pahachāntā hun

122

194.	Help, please	कृपया सहायता करें।	Kripayā sahāyatā karen
195.	Indeed.	वास्तव में।	Vāstav mein
196.	Shameful.	शर्मनाक।	Sharmanāk
197.	You can trust.	आप विश्वास कर सकते हैं।	Āp vishwās kar sakte hain
198.	Drive slow.	धीरे चलाइये।	Dhīre chalāiye
199.	Turn to left.	बायें मुड़ें।	Bāyen muren
200.	Go straight.	सीधे जायें।	Sīdhe jayen
201.	No right turn.	दायें न मुड़ें।	Dāyen na muren
202.	No 'U' turn.	यू मोड़ मना है।	'U' mor manā bai
203.	No parking.	यहां गाड़ी खड़ी न करें।	Yaban gāṛi kbrī na karen

123

204.	Exit.	बाहर।	*Bāhar*
205.	Entrance.	अन्दर।	*Andar*
206.	Private.	निजी।	*Nijī*
207.	Warning.	चेतावनी।	*Chetāvanī*
208.	Caution.	सावधानी।	*Sāvdhānī*
209.	Danger.	खतरा।	*Khatrā*
210.	Booking office.	टिकट घर।	*Tikat ghar*
211.	Inquiry office.	पूछताछ दफ्तर।	*Punchhtāchh daftar*
212.	Information centre.	सूचना केन्द्र।	*Suchanākendra*
213.	Will you prefer beer or whiskey?	आप क्या लेना पसन्द करेंगे, बियर या व्हिस्की?	*Āp kyā lenā pasand karenge Biyar yā whisk?*

124

214. Which game do you like? आप कौन सा खेल पसन्द करते हैं? *Āp konsā kbel pasand karte hain?*

215. It is very unfortunate. यह बड़े दुर्भाग्य की बात है। *Yah bare durbhagya kī bāt hai*

216. Please do not worry. कृपया चिन्ता न करें। *Kripayā chintā na karen*

217. Who lives in front of your house? आपके घर के सामने कौन रहता है ? *Āpke ghar ke sāmane kaūn rahatā hai?*

218. Who wants to talk to me? मुझसे कौन बात करना चाहता है? *Mujhse kaun bāt karanā cbābatā bai?*

219. Is there a phone for me? क्या मेरे लिए फोन है? *Kyā mere liye phone bai?*

220. Yes, there is a trunk call.   हां, ट्रंक कॉल है।   220. *Han, trunkcall hai*

221. Hold the line.   लाइन रखिये।   221. *Lāin rakhiye*

222. I am comig in a second.   मैं एक सेकिंड में आ रहा हूँ।   222. *Main ek second men ārabāhun*

223. Tell him PP is not available   उनसे कहिये पी पी नहीं है।   223. *Unse kahiye P P nahinhain*

At places 'Hindi' equivalents' to English sentences have been chosen with a view to conform to idioms and usage rather than to exactitude of translation. Masculine gender has been used in these sentences through out. Readers are requested to refer to part IV dealing in grammar, giving instructions—how to make short sentences and express themselves in Hindi.

Chapter 26
Greetings and Polite Expressions

224.	Good morning.	नमस्कार या नमस्ते	224.	*Namaskār or Namaste*
225.	Good day	नमस्कार या नमस्ते	225.	*Namaskār or Namaste*
226.	Good evening	नमस्कार या नमस्ते	226.	*Namaskār or Namaste*
227.	Good night	नमस्कार या नमस्ते	227.	*Namaskār or Namaste*
228.	Good bye	नमस्कार या नमस्ते	228.	*Namaskār or Namaste*
229.	How do you do?	आप कैसे हैं?	229.	*Āp kaise bain?*
230.	How are you?	आप कैसे हैं?	230.	*Āp kaise bain?*

231.	Are you quite well?	आप बिल्कुल अच्छी तरह हैं न?	Āp bilkul achchī tarah hain na?
232.	How are you getting on?	आपका काम कैसा चल रहा है?	Āpkā kām kaisā chal rahā hai?
233.	Quite well, thank you.	बिल्कुल ठीक, धन्यवाद।	Bilkuk thīk, dhanyavād
234.	Very well, thank you.	बहुत अच्छा, धन्यवाद।	Babut achchā, dhanyavād
235.	What is new?	नयी क्या बात है?	Nayī kyā bā bai?
236.	How are things?	क्या हाल-चाल है?	Kyā bāl-chāl hai?
237.	I am glad to see you.	मुझे आपसे मिलकर खुशी हुई	Mujbe āp se mil kar kbushī buī
238.	It is a long time since we met.	बहुत दिनों बाद मिले हैं।	Babut dinon bād mile hain since we met.

239.	How do you feel?	आपकी तबियत कैसी है?	239.	Āpki tabīyat kaisī hai?
240.	I am not quite well.	मैं बिल्कुल ठीक नहीं हूँ।	240.	Main bilkuk thīk nahīm hun
241.	How is Mr. .....?	मि0......कैसे हैं?	241.	Mr. ... kaise hain?
242.	How is Mrs. ...?	मिसेज......कैसी हैं?	242.	Mrs. ... kaisi hain?
243.	I am very pleased to meet you.	मुझे आपसे मिलकर बहुत खुशी हुई।	243.	Mujbe āp se mil kar babut kbushī buī
244.	I hope we meet again.	मैं आशा करता हूँ हम फिर मिलेंगे।	244.	Main āshā kartā hun bam pbir milengē
245.	I must go.	मुझे चलना चाहिये।	245.	Mujbe chalanā chābiye

129

246.	May I go now?	क्या, अब मैं जाऊँ?		*Kyā āb main jāun?*
247.	I am sorry to part with you but I have another engagement.	मुझे आपके पास से जाने में अफसोस है लेकिन मुझे दूसरा काम है।		*Mujbe āpke pās se jāne men afasos hai lekin mujbe dusarā kām hai*
248.	I (m) do not speak Hindi.	मैं हिन्दी नहीं बोलता।		*Main Hindi nahīn bolatā*
249.	I (m) know very little Hindi.	मैं बहुत कम हिन्दी जानता हूँ।		*Main babut kam Hindi jānatā hun*
250.	I (m) speak only English.	मैं सिर्फ अंग्रेजी बोलता हूँ।		*Main sirf Angrezī bolatāhun*
251.	I have heard a lot about you.	मैंने आपके बारे में बहुत सुना है।		*Maine āpke bāre men babut sunā hai*
252.	Allow me to introduce...	मुझे.....का परिचय कराने की आज्ञा दीजिए।		*Mube.... kā paricbay karāne kī āgyā dūnjiye*

	English	Hindi	Transliteration
253.	With pleasure.	खुशी से।	*Khushī se*
254.	Yes Sir,	जी हाँ।	*Jī han*
255.	Yes Madam.	—	—
256.	Yes Miss.	—	—
257.	No Sir.	जी नहीं।	*Jī nahīṁ*
258.	No Madam.	—	—
259.	No Miss.	—	—
260.	Please give my compliments to...	कृपया...से मेरा नमस्कार कहिये।	*Kripayā...se merā namaskār kahiye*
261.	Must yo go now?	क्या आप अब जावेंगे?	*Kyā āp ab jāvenge?*
262.	Thanks	धन्यवाद।	*Dhanyavād*
263.	Thank you	आपको धन्यवाद।	*Apko dhanyavād*
264.	Many thanks	अनेक धन्यवाद।	*Anek dhanyavād*

	English	Hindi	Transliteration
265.	I am afraid, I (m) can't stay any longer.	मुझे अफसोस है मैं और नहीं ठहर सकता।	*Mujhe afasos hai, main ab aur nahīṁ ṭhahar saktā*
266.	Much obliged.	बहुत अनुग्रहीत हूँ।	*Bahut anugrahīt hun*
267.	I am sorry, I cannot help.	मुझे खेद है, मैं आपकी सहायता नहीं कर सकता।	*Mujhe khed hai, main āpki sāhayata nahīṁ kār saktā*
268.	It can be arranged.	इसका प्रबन्ध हो सकता है।	*Iskā prabandh ho saktā hai*
269.	This is not possible.	वह सम्भव नहीं है।	*Yah Sambhav nahīṁ hai*
270.	Parking is prohibited.	वाहन खड़ा करना मना है।	*Vāhan khaṛā karnā manā hai*
271.	There is a happy news.	एक अच्छी खबर है।	*Ek achchhī khabar hai*

272.	It is a sad news.	यह दुखदाई खबर है।	*Yah dukhdaī khabar hai*
273.	No need to be angry.	नाराज होने की जरूरत नहीं।	*Nārāj hone kī zarwrat nahīṁ hai*
274.	Have patience.	सब्र से काम लो।	*Sabra se kām lo*
275.	Do not believe rumours.	अफवाहों का विश्वास मत करो।	*Afwahon kā vishwaś mat karo*

Chapter 27
Some Popular Proverbs in Hindi with English Equivalents

276. A bad man is better than bad name.

बद अच्छा बदनाम बुरा ।

276. *Bad achchhā badnam burā.*

277. A bad workman quarrels with his tools.

नाच न जाने आंगन टेढ़ा ।

277. *Nāch na jāne āngan tedhā.*

278. A bird in hand is better than two in the bush.

नौ नगद न तेरह उधार ।

278. *Nau nakad na terah udhār.*

279. A burnt child dreads the fire.

दूध का जला छाछ को फूंक कर पीता है ।

279. *Dudh kā jalā chhāchh ko phoonk kar pitā hai.*

280. A drop in the ocean.

ऊँट के मुंह में जीरा ।

280. *Unt ke munh men firā*

281.	An eye among the blind.	अन्धों में काना राजा।	281.	*Andhon men kānā rājā*
282.	A honey tongue with a heart of gall.	मुँह में राम बगल में छुरी।	282.	*Munh men Rām bagal men chhurī.*
283.	A wolf in lamb's guise.	मुँह में राम बगल में छुरी।	283.	*Munh men Rām bagal men chhurī.*
284.	A little knowledge is a dangerous thing.	अन्त भले का भला।	284.	*Ant bhale kā bhalā*
285.	An empty vessel makes much noise.	थोथा चना बाजे घना।	285.	*Thothā chanā baje ghanā*
286.	A nine day's wonder	चार दिन की चाँदनी फिर अन्धेरी रात।	286.	*Chār din kī chāndnī phir andheri rāt.*
287.	A rotten apple spoils the rest	एक गन्दी मछली सारे तालाब को गन्दा करती है।	287.	*Ek gandī machhlī sāre tālāb ko gandā kartā bai.*

135

	English	Hindi (Devanagari)	Hindi (Roman)
288.	As the king, so are the subjects.	जैसा राजा वैसी प्रजा।	*Jaisa raja waisi praja.*
289.	As you sow, so shall you reap.	जैसी करनी वैसी भरनी।	*Jaisi karni waisi bharni.*
290.	Greet is curse.	लालच बुरी बला।	*Lalach buri bala.*
291.	Barking dogs seldom bite.	जा गरजते है सो बरसते नहीं।	*Jo garijte hain so baraste nahin.*
292.	Better wear your shoes than your bed clothes.	बैठे से बेगार भली।	*Baithe se begar bhali.*
293.	Beggar and borrowers cannot be choosers.	दान की बछिया के दांत नहीं देखे जाते।	*Dan ki bachhiya ke dant nahin dekhe jate.*
294.	Between two stools we come to ground.	दुविधा में दोनें गये माया मिली न रामा।	*Duvindha men donon gaye, maya minli na Ram.*

295.	Birds of the same feather fly together.	चोर का भाई गिरह कटा।	*Chor kā bhai girha kat.*
296.	Coming events cast their shadows before.	होनहार बिरवान के होत चीकने पात।	*Honhār birwān ke hot chīkne pā̃.*
297.	Contentment is bliss.	संतोष में सबसे बड़ा सुख है।	*Santosh men sabse barā sukh hai.*
298.	Speak greek before ladies	भैंस के आगे बीन बजाना।	*Bhains ke āge bīn bajānā*
299.	Cut your coat according to your cloth.	उतने पांव पसारिये जितनी लम्बी चादर हो।	*Utne pānv pasāriye jitnī lambī chādar ho.*
300.	Diamond cuts. diamond.	लोहे को लोहा काटता है।	*Lohe ko loobā kātā hai.*
301.	Tit for tat	जैसे को तैसा	*Jaise ko taisā*
302.	Evil begets evil.	कर बुरा तो हो बुरा	*Kar būrā to ho būrā*

137

303.	Do good to forget.	नेकी कर दरिया में डाल।	303.	*Neki kar dariyā men dāl.*
304.	Drowning man catches at a straw.	डूबते को तिनके का सहारा।	304.	*Dubte ko tinke kā sahārā*
305.	Every thing is yellow to a jaundiced eye	सावन के अन्धे को हरा ही हरा दिखाई देता है।	305.	*Sāwan ke andhe ko harā hī harā dikhayī detā hai.*
306.	Ill gotten, ill spent.	जैसे आया वैसे गया।	306.	*Jaise āyā vaise gayā*
307.	Good mind, good find.	आप भला तो जग भला।	307.	*Āp bhalā to jag bhalā*
308.	Great cry little wool.	ऊंची दूकान फीका पकवान।	308.	*Unchi dukān phikā pakwān.*
309.	Guilty conscience is ever Suspicious.	चोर की दाढ़ी में तिनका।	309.	*Chor kī dāḍhī men tinkā*

138

310.	Something is better than nothing.	ना से हां भली	Nā se han bhalī.
311.	Hard nut to crack.	लोहे के चने चबाना।	Lohe ke chane chabānā
312.	High winds blow on high hills.	बड़ों की बड़ी बात।	Baron-ki batī bā.
313.	His wits are gone a wool gathering.	उसकी अक्ल चरने गई है।	Uskī akal charne gaī hai.
314.	It takes two to make a quarrel.	एक हाथ से ताली नहीं बजती।	Ek hāth se tālī nabīn bajatī.
315.	It is no use to cry over split milk	अब पछताये होत क्या जब चिड़ियाँ चुग गई खेत।	Ab pachhtaye hot kyā jab chiryan dug gai khbet.
316.	To kill two birds with one stone	एक पंथ दो काज -एक तीर से दो शिकार	Ek panth do kāj— Ek tīr se do shikār.

317.	Forget yesterdays, live todays.	बीते कल को भूल आज की सुध ले।	*Bīte kal ko bhul, aāj kī sudh le.*
318.	Like father like son.	जैसा बाप वैसा बेटा।	*Jaisā bāp waisā betā*
319.	To live from hand to mouth.	रोज कुआं खोदना, रोज पानी पीना।	*Roz kuaān khodnā, roz pānī pīnā*
320.	Make hay while the sun shines.	बहती गंगा में हाथ धोना।	*Bahtī gangā men hāāth dhonā*
321.	Man proposes, god disposes.	आदमी के चाहे क्या होता है होता वही है जो मंजूरे खुदा होता है।	*Ādmi ke chahe kyā hotā hai, hotā vahi hai jo manzure khudā hotā hai.*
322.	Many a little makes a mickle.	बूंद बूंद करके घड़ा भरता है।	*Bund bund karke gharā bhartā hai.*
323.	Many a slip between the cup and the lip.	कानी के ब्याह को नौ सो जोखिम।	*Kānī ke byāh ko nau sau jokhim.*

140

324.	Many men, many minds.	नाना मुनि नाना मति।	*Nānā muni nānā mati.*
325.	Birds of the same feather fly together.	चोर चोरे मौसेरे भाई।	*Chor chor Mausere bhāī.*
326.	Might is right.	जिसकी लाठी उसकी भैंस।	*Jiski lāṭhī uski bhains.*
327.	Misfortunes never come alone.	मुफ़लिसी में आटा गीला।	*Mufisī men çatā gīlā*
328.	Money begets money.	धन धन को कमाता है।	*Dhan dhan ko kamātā hai.*
329.	No gain without pain.	बिना सेवा मेवा नहीं मिलता।	*Binā sewā mewa nahīn miltā*
330.	One flower does not make a garland.	अकेला चना क्या भाड़ फोड़ेगा।	*Akelā chanā kyā bhāḍ foregā*
331.	Nail drives out nail.	कांटे से कांटा निकलता है।	*Kānte se kāntā nikalatā hai.*

141

332.	Out of the frying pan into the fire.	कुएं से निकला खाई में गिरा।
333.	Penny wise pound foolish.	जान जाये दमड़ी न जाये।
334.	As you sow, so shall you reap.	जैसा करोगे वैसा भरोगे।
335.	Truth has no fear.	सांच को आंच नहीं।
336.	Riches have wings.	लक्ष्मी चंचल होती है।
337.	Respect begets respect.	अपनी इज्जत अपने हाथ।
338.	Rome was not built in a day.	हथेली पर सरसों नहीं उगती।

332. *Kuyen se nikalā khaī̃ men girā*

333. *Jān jāye damdī na jāye.*

334. *Jaisā karoge waisā bharoge.*

335. *Sānch ko ānch nachī̃.*

336. *lakshmī chanchal hotī hai.*

337. *Apnī izzat apne hāth.*

338. *Hathelī par sason nahī̃ ugatī.*

339.	Time once lost is never regained.	गया समय कभी नहीं लौटता।	*Gayā samay kabhī nahīṁ lautatā*	339.
340.	Selfpraise carries no recommendation.	अपने मुंह मियां मिट्ठू बनने से काम नहीं चलता।	*Apne munh miyāṁ mittḥu banene se kām nahīṁ chalatā*	340.
341.	Take opportunity.	अवसर का लाभ उठाओ।	*Avsar kā lābh uṭhāo.*	341.
342.	Crying in wilderness.	भैंस के आगे बीन बजाना।	*Bhains ke āge bīn bajānā*	342.
343.	Only the wearer knows where the shoe pinches swine.	जाके तन न फटी बिवाई, सो क्या जाने पीर पराई।	*Jāke tan na phatī biwāī, so kyā jane pīr parāi.*	343.
344.	To cast pearls before swine	बन्दर क्या जाने अदरक का स्वाद।	*Bandar kyā jāne adrak kā swād.*	344.
345.	To make mountain of a mole-hill.	राई का पर्वत बनाना, तिल का ताड़ बनाना।	*Rāī kā parvat bānanā, til kā tāḍ banānā*	345.

143

346.	To make castles in the air.	हवाई किले बनाना।	Havā̃ kile banānā
347.	Too many cooks spoil the broth.	बहुत से जोगी मठ उजाड़ें।	Bahut se jogi math ujāṛen.
348.	Unity is stength.	एकता ही बल है।	Ekatā hi bal hai.
349.	To rob Peter to pay Paul.	गाय मार कर जूता दान।	Gāy mār kar jutā dān.
350.	Live and let others live.	जिओ और जिने दो।	Jīo aur jīne do.
351.	To take coals to New Castle.	उल्टे बांस बरेली को।	Ultē bans barelī ko.
352.	A man is known by his actions and not words.	आदमी कर्म से बनता है बातों से नहीं।	Ādmi karam se bantā hai bāton se nabīm.
353.	Poverty is a curse.	गरीबी एक अभिशाप है।	Garībī ek abbishāp hai.

354.	Love is a blessing.	प्यार एक वरदान है।	_Pyār ek vardān hai._
355.	Pride goes before a fall.	घमण्ड का सिर नीचा।	_Ghamand kā sir nīchā_
356.	Knowledge is power.	ज्ञान शक्ति है।	_Gyān shakti hai._
357.	Hope sustains life.	आशा जीवन की आत्मा है।	_Āsha jīvan kī ātmā hai._
358.	To throw dust in one's eye.	आँखों में धूल डालना।	_Ānkhon men dhul dālnā_
359.	Dearest pupil of one's eye.	आँख का तारा।	_Ānkh kā tārā_
360.	To indulge in tall talks. (Gossip)	लम्बी चौड़ी हांकना।	_Lambī chaurī hānknā_
361.	Without sweat no pleasure.	बिना मरे स्वर्ग नहीं मिलता।	_Binā mare swarg nahīn miltā_

145

362.	Prevention is better than cure.	परहेज इलाज से बेहतर है।	362. *Parhez ilāj se behtar hai.*
363.	Whistling maid and crowing hen are neither fit for gods nor men.	धोबी का कुत्ता, घर का न घाट का।	363. *Dhobī kā kuttā ghar kā nā ghāṭ kā*
364.	Craft or cunning is ever courteous.	दगा बाजी सदा मीठा बोलती है।	364. *Dagābāzī sadā mīṭhā boltī hai.*
365.	Falsehood has no roots.	चोर के पैर नहीं होते।	365. *Chor ke pair nahīṅ hote.*
366.	Vice is a winning harlot.	बुराई एक मोहक स्त्री है।	366. *Burai ek mohak strī hai.*
367.	Without head and tail.	बे सिर पैर की।	367. *Be sir pair kī.*
368.	Between devil and deep sea.	इधर कुआं उधर खाई।	368. *Idhar kuan, udhar khai.*
369.	Health is a blessing.	तन्दरुस्ती हजार नियामत।	369. *Tandrustī hazār niyāmat.*

370.	Fortune favours the brave.	भाग्य वीरों का साथी।	Bhāgya vīrron kā sāthī.
371.	Example is better than precept.	उपदेश करने से स्वयं करना भला।	Updesh karne se swayam karnā bhalā
372.	Discontent is the mother of revolt.	असन्तोष क्रान्ति को जन्म देता है।	Asantosh krānti ko Janm detā bai.
373.	Sow thistles and expect pickles.	बोया पेड़ बबूल का, आम कहां से खायं।	Boyā per babul kā, ām kahān sēkhaye.
374.	Speak Greek before ladies.	मूर्ख के आगे रोये अपने नयन खोये।	Murkh ke āge roye āpne nayan kboye.
375.	Beauty needs no ornaments.	सुन्दरता को आभूषण की आवश्यकता नहीं।	Sundartā ko abbushan ki awāśbyaktā nabīm
376.	God sees the truth but waits.	ईश्वर के घर देर है पर अन्धेर नहीं।	Ishwar ke ghar der hai par andber nabīm.

147

Apologies

377.	I (m) beg your pardon.	मैं आपसे माफ़ी चाहता हूँ।	377. *Main āpse māfī chhāetā hun*
378.	Excuse me please.	कृपया मुझे क्षमा करें।	378. *Kripayā mujhe kshamā karen*
379.	Excuse me, I (m) should like to ask.	माफ़ कीजिए, मैं पूछना चाहता हूँ।	379. *Māf kījiye main puchchanā chāhatā hun*
380.	Please excuse my pronunication.	मेरे अशुद्ध उच्चारण को क्षमा करें।	380. *Mere ashuddh uchchāran ko incorrect kshamā karen*
381.	Forgive me for being late.	माफ़ कीजिए, मुझे देर हो गई।	381. *Māf kījiye mujhe der ho gai*

148

382.	Forgive me for. interrupting	बीच में बोलने के लिए मुझे माफ करें।	*Bīch men bolane ke liye mujhe māf karen*
383.	Forgive me for. coming in between	बीच में आने के लिए मुझे माफ करें।	*Bīch men āne ke liye mujhe māf karen*
384.	For give me for not telephoning.	मैं टेलीफोन नहीं कर सका, कृपया माफ करें।	*Main telephone nahīn kar saka, kripayā māf karen*
385.	I am so sorry.	मुझे बहुत अफसोस है।	*Mujhe bahut afsos hai*
386.	Sorry, this was by mistake.	मुझे अफसोस है। यह मेरी गलती है	*Mujhe afsos hai, yah merī galatī thī*
387.	It does not matter	कोई बात नहीं।	*Koī bāt nahīn*
388.	There is no harm done.	कोई हानि नहीं हुई।	*Koī hāni nahīn huī*

389.	Make my apologies.	मेरी ओर से माफी मांग लीजिए।	Merī̃or se māfī mang lījiye
390.	No apology is needed.	माफी की कोई जरूरत नहीं।	Māfī̃kī koī̃zarurat nahī̃
391.	Do not apologise..	माफी न मांगिए	Māfī̃na māngiye
392.	Not in the least.	बिल्कुल नहीं।	Bilkul nahī̃
393.	Can I be of any service to you?	क्या मैं आपकी कोई सेवा कर सकता हूँ।	Kyā main āpkī̃koī̃ sevā kar sakata bun?
394.	Can I be of any help to you?.	क्या मैं आपकी कोई सहायता कर सकता हूँ।	Kyā main āpkī̃koī̃ sāyatā kār saktā bun
395.	It was not my fault.	यह मेरा कसूर नहीं था।	Yab merā kasur nahī̃ thā
396.	It was not your fault.	यह आपका कसूर नहीं था।	Yab āpkā kasur nahī̃ thā

397. It was my mistake.

यह गलती से हो गया।

Yah galtī se ho gayā

398. I took your (news) paper by mistake, I thought it was mine.

मैंने आपका अखबार गलती से ले लिया, मैं समझा मेरा था।

Maine āpkā akhbār galtī se le liya main samajha merā thā

399. I entered your room. by mistake; I thought it was mine.

मैं गलती से आपके कमरे में घुस गया, मैं समझा मेरा था।

Main galtī se āpke kamare men ghus gayā; main samajhā merā thā

151

Chapter 28
Wishes

400.	What do you want?	आप क्या चाहते हैं?	*Āp kyā chhāte hain?*
401.	I (m) want a room.	मैं एक कमरा चाहता हूँ।	*Main ek kamrā chāhatā hun*
402.	I (m) want breakfast.	मैं ब्रेकफास्ट चाहता हूँ।	*Main breakfāst chāhatā hun*
403.	I (m) want to rest.	मैं आराम करना चाहता हूँ।	*Main ārām karanā chāhatā hun*
404.	I (m) want to go to the market.	मैं बाजार जाना चाहता हूँ।	*Main bāzār jānā chāhatā hun*
405.	I (m) want to go to the cinema.	मैं सिनेमा जाना चाहता हूँ।	*Main cinemā jana chāhatā hun*
406.	I (m) want to see a good film.	मैं अच्छी फिल्म देखना चाहता हूँ।	*Main achchhī film dekhnā chāhatā hun*

152

Chapter 29
Washerman

407. Where is the complaint book?

शिकायत की किताब कहाँ है?

407. *Shikāyat kī kitab kabān hai?*

408. Have my bill sent to me by the evening.

मेरा बिल शाम तक मेरे पास पहुँचवा दीजिये।

408. *Merā bil shām tak mere paās pahunchwā dījye*

409. I shall pay the bill.

मैं बिल चुका दूँगा।

409. *Main bil chukā dungā*

410. Do you accept cheques?

क्या आप चेक ले लेते हैं?

410. *Kyā āp chek le lete hain?*

411. No, we accept only cash.

नहीं, हम केवल नकद लेते हैं।

411. *Nahīm, ham kewal nakas lete hain?*

153

412. Please call the washerman. कृपया धोबी को बुलाइये। *kripayā dhobī ko bulāiye*

413. Will you dryclean the woollen suit? क्या आप इस ऊनी सूट को ड्राइक्लीन करा देंगे ? *Kyā āp is ūnī sut ko drāklīn karā dange?*

414. What are the charges? इसका कितना लेंगे ? *Iskā kitnā lenge?*

415. Please get my suit pressed. कृपया मेरा सूट प्रेस करवा दे। *Kripayā merā sut pres karawā den*

416. Please get my overcoat cleaned. कृपया मेरा ओवरकोट साफ़ करवा दे *Kripayā merā ovarkot sāf karawā den*

417. —dress— —ड्रेस— *...dres.....*

418. —shirt— —कमीज़— *....KamŪz.....*

419. —skirt— —स्कर्ट— *.....Skart.....*

420. —jacket— —जैकिट— *.....Jaikit.....*

154

421. I want these things washed. मैं इन चीजों को धुलवाना चाहता हूँ। 421. Main in chīzon ko dhulawānd chāhtā hun.

422. You must bring back this evening. इसको आप शाम को ज़रूर वापिस ले आइये 422. Isko āp shām ko zarur wāpis le āye

423. You have not put enough starch in it. इसमें आपने काफी कलफ़ नहीं लगायी है 423. Ismen āpne kāfī kalaf nahīn lāgāi hai

424. You must take it back. आप इसको वापिस ले जाइये। 424. Āp isko wāpis le jāiye

425. You have scorched this dress. आपने इस ड्रेस को जला दिया है। 425. Āpne is dress ko jalā diyā hai

426. You have put too much blue in my white shirt. आपने मेरे सफेद कमीज़ में बहुत नील डाल दी है। 426. Āpne mere safed kamīj men babut nil dāl dī hai

155

427. When will you (m)
return these clothes?

आप यह कपड़े कब लौटावेंगे?

*Āp yah kapare
kab lauṭevenge?*

428. Have you counted them?

क्या आपने इन्हें गिन लिया है?

*Kyā āpne inhen gin
liyā hai?*

429. Have you made a list?

क्या आपने सूची बना ली है?

*Kyā āpne suchi banā
lī hai?*

430. Will you (m) give me
a copy of the list?

क्या आप सूची की
एक नकल देंगे?

*Kyā aāp suchī kī ek
nakal denge?*

431. I shall give by this night.

मैं आज रात तक दे दूँगा।

*Main aāj rat tak de
dūngā*

432. I shall give by .
tomorrow morning

कल सेवरे तक

Kal sabare tak

156

433.	I shall give by tomorrow evening.	मैं कल शाम तक दे दूँगा।
434.	You have not washed well.	आपने अच्छी तरह नहीं धोया है।
435.	You have not ironed well.	आपने अच्छी तरह इस्त्री नहीं की है।
436.	You have torn the shirt.	आपने कमीज फाड़ दिया है।
437.	You have torn the coat.	—कोट—
438.	You have torn the pair of trousers.	—पतलून—
439.	I want to have my shoes repaired.	मैं अपने जूतों की मरम्मत कराना चाहता हूँ।

433.	*Main kal shām tak de dungā*
434.	*Āpne achchī tarah nahīṁ dhoyā hai*
435.	*Āpne achchbī tarah istrī nahīṁ kī hai*
436.	*Āpne kamīj fāṛ diyā hai*
437.	*—Kot—*
438.	*—Patlun—*
439.	*Main āpme jūton kī marammat karānā chāhatā bun*

157

440. I want to have my shoes polished.

मैं अपने जूतों पर पालिश कराना चाहता हूँ।

440. Main āpne jutton par pŏlish kārānā chahatā hun

441. I want a pair of strings for my shoes.

मैं अपने जूतों के लिए दो फीते चाहता हूँ।

441. Main āpne jutton ke liye do fīte chāhatā hun

158

Chapter 30

Breakfast, Lunch and Dinner

442.	Have you had breakfast?	आपने नाश्ता कर लिया?
443.	Not yet. Let us have breakfasttogether.	अभी नहीं। हम लोग एक साथ नाश्ता करें।
444.	Is breakfast ready?	क्या नाश्ता तैयार है?
445.	The breakfast is ready.	नाश्ता तैयार है।
446.	Do you want tea, coffee or cocoa?	आप चाय चाहते हैं या या कॉफी या कोको?
447.	A cup of tea.	एक प्याला चाय का।

442.	*Āpne nāstā kar liyā?*
443.	*Abhī'nahīṅ, hum log ek sāth nāshtā karen*
444.	*Kyā nāshtā taiyār hai?*
445.	*Nāstā taiyār hai*
446.	*Āp chāy chāhte hain yā Kaufī ya koko?*
447.	*Ek pyālā chāy kā*

448.	A cup of coffee.	एक प्याला कौफी का।	*Ek pyālā kaufī kā*
449.	Do you take your coffee black or with cream?	आप काली कौफी लेते हैं या क्रीम के साथ?	*Āp kālī kaufī lete hain yā krīm ke sāth?*
450.	Do you take your tea with sugar? or without sugar.	आप चाय में चीनी लेते हैं या बिना चीनी की?	*Āp chāy men chīnī lete bain yā binā chīnī ki?*
451.	Do you take one lump of sugar?	क्या आप चीनी की एक डली लेते हैं?	*Kyā āp chīnī ke ek dalī lete bain?*
452.	No, I take two.	नहीं, मैं दो लेता हूँ।	*Nabīn, main do letā bun*
453.	Tea for one..	एक जाने के लिए चाय।	*Ek jāne ke liye chāy*
454.	Tea for two.	दो जाने के लिए चाय।	*Do jane ke liye chāy*

160

455.	We want more cups	हमें और प्याले चाहिये।	Hamen aur pyāle chāhiye
456.	Pour out tea.	चाय डालिये	Chāy dāliye
457.	Do you like it strong?.	क्या आप तेज चाय पसन्द करते हैं?	Kyā āp tej chāy pasand karate hain?
458.	No.	नहीं।	Nahīn
459.	Is your tea sweet enough?	आपकी चाय मीठी हो गई?	Āpkī chāy mīthī gaī?
460.	Another cup of tea.	चाय का एक प्याला और।	Chāy kā ek pyālā aur
461.	Rather too strong.	तेज अधिक है।	Tej adhik hai
462.	I like weak tea.	मुझे हलकी चाय पसन्द है।	Mujhe halkī chāy pasand hai

463.	Please ring the bell.	कृपया घंटी बजाइये।	*Kripayā ghantī bajāiye*
464.	A little more milk.	थोड़ा और दूध।	*Thorā aur dudb*
465.	Some bread and butter.	थोड़ी रोटी और मक्खन।	*Thorī rotī aur makkhan*
466.	A small piece.	एक छोटा टुकड़ा	*Ek chhotā tukrā*
467.	Please pass me the milk jug.	कृपया दूध का बर्तन दीजिये।	*Kripayā dudb kā bartan dījiyē*
468.	Pleaese pass me the cream.	कृपया क्रीम दीजिये।	*Kripayā krm dījiye*
469.	Please pass me the sugar.	कृपया चीनी दीजिये।	*Kripayā chīnī dījiye*
470.	Please pass me the salt.	कृपया नमक दीजिये।	*Kripayā namak dījiye*
471.	Please bring us some pastries.	कृपया हमारे लिये कुछ पेस्ट्री लाइये।	*Kripayā hamare liye kuchh pestrī lāiye*

162

	English	Hindi (Devanagari)	Romanized
472.	Please bring us some biscuits.	—बिस्कुट—	—Biscūṭ—
473.	Please bring us some cake.	—केक—	—Kek—
474.	This cream is sour.	यह क्रीम खट्टी है।	Yah creām khaṭṭī hai
475.	Give me some fresh butter.	मुझे थोड़ा ताजा मक्खन दीजिये।	Mujhe thorā tājā makkhan dājiye
476.	Thus butter is stale	मक्खन बासी है।	Makkahn bāsī hai
477.	Bring some more.	थोड़ा और लाइये।	Thorā aur lāiye
478.	Take it away.	यह ले जाइये।	Yah le jāiye
479.	A little more fish.	थोड़ी और मछली	Thorī aur machhalī
480.	Yes, please.	जी हाँ, कृपया	Jī han, kripayā
481.	A little more.	थोड़ा और।	Thorā aur

163

482.	Nothing More.	अब कुछ नहीं।	482. *Ab kuchh nahīṁ*
483.	We will take our breakfast in our room.	हम अपना नाश्ता अपने कमरे में करेंगे।	483. *Ham āpna nāstā apne kamaremeṁ karenge*
484.	Please bring us some fruit.	हमारे लिये कुछ फल लाइये।	484. *Hamāre liye kuch phal lāiye*
485.	Bring me the bill.	कृपया अपना बिल लाइये।	485. *Kripayā apnā bil lāiye*
486.	Where is a good restaurant here.	यहाँ अच्छा रेस्टोरेन्ट कहाँ है?	486. *Yahan achchhā restorant kahan hai?*
487.	Waiter	वेटर	487. *Weter*
488.	What time is lunch?	लंच कै बजे होता है?	488. *Lanch kai baje botā hai?*

164

	English	Hindi (Devanagari)	Hindi (Romanized)
489.	Is lunch ready?	क्या लंच (दोपहर का खाना) तैयार है?	Kyā lunch (dophāhar kā khānā) thaiyar hai?
490.	What time is dinner?	रात का खाना कै बजे होता है?	Rāt kā khānā kai baje botā hai?
491.	What time do you finish dinner?	रात का खाना कै बजे खत्म होता है?	Rāt kā khānā kai baje khatm hotā hain?
492.	What is the price?	क्या कीमत है?	Kyā kīmat hai?
493.	Do you charge separately for each dish?	क्या हरेक प्लेट के लिये अलग अलग दाम लेते हैं?	Kyā barek plet ke liye alag alag dām lete hai?
494.	Is wine included?	क्या उसमें शराब शामिल है?	Kyā usmen sharāb shamil hai?
495.	We shall lunch at 1-30 p.m.	हम दोपहर को डेढ़ बजे लंच करेंगे।	Ham dopahar ko dedh boje lanch karenge

165

496. We shall dinner at 9 p.m. हम रात को नौ बजे खाना खावेंगे। *Ham rāt-ko nau baje khānā khāvenge*

497. What soup will you have? आप कौन सा सूप लेंगे? *Āp kaun sā sup lenge?*

498. Will you take some soup? क्या आप थोड़ा सूप लेंगे? *Kyā āp thorā sup lenge?*

499. Help yourself. खाने में से लीजिये। *Khāne mn se lijiye*

500. It is excellent. यह बहुत बढ़िया है। *Yah bahut badhiyā hai*

501. Give me another fork and knife. मुझे दूसरा काँटा और छुरी दीजिये। *Mujhe dusrā kantā aur chhuri dījiye*

502. This spoon is not clean. यह चम्मच साफ नहीं है। *Yah chammach sāf nahīn hai*

503.	Change the plates please.	कृपया प्लेट बदलिये।	Kripayā plet badliye
504.	I want another napkin.	मुझे दूसरा नेपकिन चाहिये।	Mujhe dusrā nepkin chāhiye
505.	What wine will you have?	आप कौन सी शराब लेंगे ?	Āp kaun sī sharab lenge?
506.	Give me the list.	मुझे सूची दीजिये।	Mujhe sūchi dījiye
507.	Here is the list.	यह सूची है।	Yah sūchi hai
508.	I will have a peg of wine.	मैं शराब का एक पेग लूंगा।	Main shārab kā ek peg lungā
509.	–half a peg of—	–आधा पेग—	–ādhā peg—
510.	–a bottle of—	–एक बोतल—	–Ek botal–
511.	What sweet dishes have you?	आपके पास मीठी क्या चीज़ें हैं ?	Āpke pās mīṭhī kya chījēn hai?
512.	Do you smoke?	क्या आप धूम्रपान करते हैं ?	Kyā āp dhumrapān karte hai?

167

513.	Do you want a packet of cigarettes?	क्या आपको सिगरेट का एक पैकेट चाहिये ?	513.	*Kyā āpko cigaret kā ek paiket chāhiye?*
514.	Which brand?	कौन से मार्के का ?	514.	*Kaunse marke kā?*
515.	I prefer a cigar.	मैं सिगार अधिक पसन्द करता हूँ।	515.	*Main cigār adhik pasand kartā hun*
516.	What meat dishes have you?	आपके पास मांस की क्या चीजें हैं ?	516.	*Āpke pās mans ki kyā kyā chīzen hain?*
517.	Are you a vegetarian?	क्या आप शाकाहारी हैं ?	517.	*Kyā āp shākāhārī hain?*
518.	No. I am a non-vegetarian.	नहीं, मैं मांसाहारी हूँ।	518.	*Nabīn main mansāhārī bun*
519.	What vegetables do you have ?	आपके पास सब्जियाँ क्या है ?	519.	*Āpke pās sabjiyan kyā kyā bain?*

168

520. Do you serve curd?

क्या आप दही परोसते हैं?

520. *Kyā āp dahī paroste bain?*

521. No, we have some preparations of curd.

नहीं, हमारे पास दही की कुछ तैयारियां हैं।

521. *Nahīṃ, hamāre pās dahī ki kūchh taiyāriyan bain*

Chapter 31

Visiting Friend

522. Tell me please where is house number twenty on this road.

कृपया मुझे बतादये कि इस सड़क पर मकान नम्बर बीस कहाँ है।

Kripayā mujhe batāiye ki is sarak par makan nambar bīs kahan hai

523. I am a foreigner and do not know the town.

मैं विदेशी हूँ और इस शहर से वाकिफ नहीं हूँ।

Main wideshi hun air is shahr se wākif nahīn hun

524. I have lost my way.

मैं रास्ता भूल गया हूँ।

Main rastā bbul gayā hun

525. Where is the... market?

...बाजार कहाँ हैं?

...Bāzār kahan hai?

526. I shall show the way to you.

मैं आप को रास्ता दिखला दूँगा।

Main āpko rāsta dikkhalā dungā

527.	Which direction?	किस दिशा में ?	Kis dishā men?
528.	Which road?	कौन सी सड़क ?	Kaunsī sarak?
529.	Where is the petrol pump?	पेट्रोल पंप कहां है।	Petrol pamp kahan hai?
530.	Where is the tax stand?	टैक्सी स्टैंड कहाँ है ?	Taxi stand kahan hai?
531.	Be so kind as to tell me how to get to the railway station	मुझे यह बतलाने की कृपा कीजिये कि मैं रेलवे स्टेशन कैसे पहुँचू?	Mujhe yah batlāne ki kripā kījiye ki main railway station kaise pahunchun?
532.	Where is the .... cinema?	...सिनेमा कहाँ है ?	...cinema kahan hai?
533.	Where is the public convenience?	पेशाब घर कहाँ है ?	Peshāb ghar kahan hai?

171

534. I want the house to...... मैं ...मकान चाहता हूँ। *Main ... makān chāhtā bun?*

535. Do you know Mr....? क्या आप मिस्टर...को जानते हैं? *Kyā āp mistar ...ko jānte bai?*

536. I do not know anyone of this name. मैं इस नाम के किसी आदमी को नहीं जानता। *Main is nām ke kisi admi ko nahīṁ jāntā*

537. I know him. मैं उनको जानता हूँ। *Main unko jāntā bun*

538. One lady wants to see you. एक महिला आप से मिलना चाहती हैं। *Ek mahilā āpse milna chāhtī bai*

539. When could I see him/her? मैं उनसे अब मिल सकता हूँ। *Main urse kab mil saktā bun?*

540. Could you come again? क्या आप फिर आ सकते है ? *Kyā āp fir ā sakte bain?*

541.	I(m) shall call tomorrow.	मैं कल आऊँगा।	541.	*Main kal aungā*
542.	I (f) shall call tomorrow.	मैं कल आऊँगी।	542.	*Main kal aungī*
543.	What name shall I say?	मैं क्या नाम बताऊँ?	543.	*Main kyā nām batāūṁ?*
544.	Mrs. Bhatia is not at home.	मिसेज़ भाटिया घर पर नहीं है।	544.	*Mrs. Bhatia ghar par nahīṁ bain*
545.	How is Mrs.....?	मिसेज़ .....कैसी हैं?	545.	*Mrs. ... kaisī bain?*
546.	I must go now.	मुझे अब चलना चाहिये।	546.	*Mujhe ab chalnā chāiye*
547.	Must you go soon?	क्या आप इतनी जल्दी चले जावेंगे?	547.	*Kyā āp itnī jaldi chale jawāṅge?*
548.	I wish you goodnight.	आपको नमस्कार।	548.	*Āpko namaskār*
549.	Good bye.	विदा, नमस्कार	549.	*Vidā, namaskār*

173

550.	Which bus goes to...?	....को कौन सी बस जाती है?
551.	Route number 29.	उनतीस नंबर की बस।
552.	Please tell me which bus I should take to reach...?	कृपया मुझे बताला‌इये कि.....पहुँचने के लिए मुझे कौन सी बस लेनी चाहिये।
553.	Route number 4, 9, 21 Or 35.	बस नंबर 4, 9, 21, या 35.
554.	Will it stop near...?	क्या वह....ठहरेगी?
555.	A little way from...	....से थोड़ी दूर।
556.	Then you can walk.	तब आप पैदल जा सकते है।

550.	.. ko kaun si bus jatī hai?
551.	Unīs number kī bus
552.	kripayā mujhe bātalāiye ki... pahunchane ke liye mujhe kaunsī bas lenī chahiye?
553.	Bus No. 4, 9, 21, yā 35
554.	Kyā wah... thatharegī?
555.	... Se thorī dur
556.	Tab āp paidal jā sakte bain

174

557.	It is a short distance from there.	वह वहां से थोड़ी दूर है।	557.	Wah wahn se thodī dur hai
558.	The bus is very crowded.	बस से बहुत भीड़ है।	558.	Bus men bahut bhīr hai
559.	There is not even standing accommodation.	खड़े होने की भी जगह नहीं है।	559.	Khare hone k– bhi jagah nabīn hai
560.	People do not stand in Q.	आदमी Q में खड़े नहीं होते।	560.	Ādmī Q men khare nabīn hote
561.	People break the Q.	लोग Q को तोड़ देते है।	561.	Log Q ko tor dete hain
562.	They rush.	वे आगे झपटते है।	562.	Ve āe jhaptate hain
563.	They push.	वे धक्का देते हैं।	563.	Ve dhakkā dete hain

175

564. They elbow.

वे कुहनी मारते हैं।

564. *Ve kuhanī mārte hain*

565. Bombay's bus service is better than Delhi's.

दिल्ली के बजाय मुम्बई की बस सर्विस अच्छी है।

565. *Delhi ke bajāy Bombay kī bus sercvice acbchhī bai*

566. Delhi bus service is hopeless.

दिल्ली बस सर्विस की दुर्दशा है।

566. *Delhi bus service kī durdashā bai*

Chapter 32
Shopping

567.	I want a pair of socks.	मुझे एक जोड़ी मोजे चाहिये।
		Mujhe ek jorī moje chāhiye
568.	Do you guarantee?	क्या आप गारंटी करते हैं?
		Kyā āp garanti karte hain?
569.	Can you tell me?	क्या आप मुझे बता सकते हैं?
		Kyā āp mujhe batā sakte hain?
570.	Where shall I buy?	मैं कहाँ खरीदूँ?
		Main kahan kharidun?
571.	Is the shop far away?	क्या वह दुकान दूर है?
		Kyā vah dukān dur hai?
572.	Have you any....?	क्या आपके पास है....?
		Kyā āpke pās....hai?

573.	What is this a metre?	एक मीटर की क्या कीमत है?
574.	How much for a pair?	एक जोड़े की क्या कीमत है?
575.	How much for a dozen?	—दर्जन—
576.	How much for a score?	—कोड़ी—
577.	How much for a hundred?	—सौ—
578.	How much for a thousand?	—हजार—
579.	I want a shirt, which colour is white.	मुझे एक कमीज चाहिये जिसका रंग सफेद हो।
580.	Show me some....	मुझे कुछ ....दिखाइये।
581.	I wish to buy....	मुझे कुछ खरीदना .... चाहता हूँ।

573.	Ek mītar ki kyā kīmat hai?
574.	Ek jore kī kyā kīmat hai?
575.	—Darjan—
576.	—Korī—
577.	—Sau—
578.	—Hazār—
579.	Mujhe ek kamīj chahiye jiskā rang safed ho
580.	Mujhe kuchh.. dikhāie
581.	Main kuchh.... kharīdnā chāhtā hun.

178

582.	What is the price?	क्या कीमत है?	Kyā kīmat hai?
583.	How much for it?	इसके कितने ?	Iske kitne?
584.	That is too much.	वह बहुत ज्यादा है।	Vah bahut jyādā hai
585.	It the price fixed?	क्या एक दाम है?	Kyā ek dām hai?
586.	Will you give is for ten rupees?	क्या आप यह दस रुपये में देंगे?	Kyā āp yab das rupaye men denge?
587.	State your minimum price	कम से कम कितने में देंगे ?	Kam se kam kitne men denge?
588.	Will the colour not run out?	रंग तो इसका नहीं निकल जाएगा ?	Rang to iskā nahīn nikal jāyegā?
589.	Send it to my house.	इसको मेरे घर भेज दीजिये।	Isko mere ghar bhek dijiye
590.	To what name?	किस नाम पर?	Kis nām par?
591.	To Which address?	किस पते पर ?	Kis pate par?

179

592.	Can you recommend a good shop?	क्या आप अच्छी दुकान बतला सकते हैं?	Kyā āp achchhī dukan batla sakate hain?
593.	It is quite reliable.	यह बिल्कुल विश्वास के योग्य है।	Yah bilkul vishwāsh ke yogya hai
594.	This will do?	यह ठीक है।	Yah thīk hai
595.	Do you keep....?	क्या आपके पास...हैं?	Kyā āpke pās... hai?
596.	Do you have....?	क्या आपके पास ...हैं?	Kyā āpke pās... hai?
596.	May we get it for you?	क्या आपके लिए हम मंगा दें।	Kyā āpke liye ham mangā den?
597.	I will try another shop.	मैं दूसरी दुकान में देखूंगा।	Main dusrī dukān men dekhungā
598.	I can get it cheaper at the other shop.	मैं दूसरी दुकान में इससे सस्ता खरीद सकता हूं।	Main dusrī dukan men isse sastā kharid saktā hun

180

599.	The other shop was quoting only eight rupees.	दूसरी दुकान वाला सिर्फ आठ रुपये कह रहा था।	599.	*Dusrī dukān wālā sirf ātḥ rupaye kaḥ rabā thā*
600.	I do not want this.	मुझे यह नहीं चाहिये।	600.	*Muḥe yaḥ nahīn chāhiye*
601.	Show me another variety.	मुझे और मेल दिखाइये।	601.	*Mujhe aur mel dikḥāiyte*
602.	Not so costly.	इतना कीमती नहीं।	602.	*Itnā kīmati nabīn*
603.	I want a cheaper one.	मुझे इससे सस्ता चाहिये।	603.	*Mujhe isse sastā chāhiye*
604.	I do not want this colour.	मुझे इस रंग का नहीं चाहिये।	604.	*Mujhe is rang kā nabīn chaḥiye*
605.	Not so dark.	इतना गहरा नहीं।	605.	*Itnā gabrā nabīn*
606.	Of a ligher shade.	इससे हल्का रंग का।	606.	*Isse balkā rang kā*

607.	It is faded.	इसका रंग उड़ा हुआ है।	Iskā rang urā buā hai
608.	Not so coarse.	इतना मोटा नहीं।	Itnā motā nahīṃ
609.	Not so fine.	इतना बारीक नहीं।	Itnā bārīk nahīṃ
610.	This is good.	यह अच्छा है।	Yab achchhā bai
611.	It is very dear.	यह बहुत महंगा है।	Yab bahut mahangā bai
612.	Quite cheap.	बिल्कुल सस्ता।	Bilkul sastā
613.	It appears old.	यह पुराना मालूम पड़ता है।	Yab puranā mālum partā bai
614.	I want a new one.	मुझे नया चाहिये।	Mujhe nayā chāhiye
615.	Will it shrink?	क्या यह सिकुड़ेगा?	Kyā yab sikuṛegā?
616.	Will it wash?	क्या यह धुल सकेगा?	Kyā yab dbul sakegā?

182

617.	This is rotten.	यह सड़ा है।	Yah sarā hai
618.	This is over-ripe.	यह अधिक पका है।	Yah adhik pakā hai
619.	This is raw.	यह कच्चा है।	Yah kachchā hai
620.	This is not yet ripe.	यह अभी पका नहीं है।	Yah abhi pakā nahīn hai
621.	This is stale.	यह बासी है।	Yah bāsī hai
622.	I want fresh.	मैं ताजा चाहता हूँ।	Main tājā chāhtā hun
623.	Where is the order counter?	ऑर्डर देने का काउन्टर कौन सा है?	Order dene kā kauntar kaunsā hai?
624.	Please take an order.	कृपया ऑर्डर लीजिये।	Kripayā order lījiye
625.	Please write down the order.	कृपया ऑर्डर लीखिये।	Kripayā order līkhiye

183

626.	Where is the packing counter?	पैक करने का काउन्टर कहाँ हैं?	Pack karene kā kāuntar kaban hai?
627.	Wrap the articles.	इन चीजों को लपेट दीजियें	In chījon ko lapet dījiye
628.	Which is the payment counter?	दाम देने का काउन्टर कौन सा हैं?	Dām dene kā kāuntar kaunsā hai
629.	Please deliver them to me.	कृपया उन्हें मुझे दे दीजियें।	Kripayā umben mujeb de dījiye
630.	Where is my bill?	मेरा बिल कहां हैं?	Merā bill kabm hai?
631.	How much do I pay?	मुझे कितना देना हैं?	Mujhe kitnā denā hai

184

632.	Please deliver the goods at my hotel.	कृपया ये सामान मेरे होटल में पहुँचवा दीजिये।	632.	*Kripcyā ye sāmān mere hotel men pahunchawā dījiye*
633.	What is the address?	पता क्या है ?	633.	*Patā kyā hai?*
634.	To whom it be delivered?	यह किसको देना है ?	634.	*Yah kisko denā hai?*
635.	To what name?	किस नाम पर ?	635.	*Kis nām par?*
636.	Will they pay there or will you pay here?	दाम वहाँ वे देंगे या आप यहाँ देंगे ?	626.	*Dām wahan we denge, yā āp yaban denge?*
637.	Do you allow any discount?	आप कोई कमीशन काटते है ?	637.	*Āp koī kamīshan kāṭate hain?*
638.	Will you show the discount on the bill?.	क्या आप बिल में कमीशन कम कर देंगे ?	638.	*Kyā āp bill men kamīshan kam kar denge?*

Chapter 33

Travel by Train and Air

639. How long does the train stop at the railway station?　स्टेशन पर गाड़ी कितनी देर ठहरती है?　639. *Station par garī kitnī der thahartī hai?*

640. Is it a mail train?　क्या यह डाक गाड़ी है?　640. *Kyā yah ḍāk garī hai?*

641. Is it an express train?　एक्सप्रेस　641. *—Express—*

642. Is it an passenger train?　पैसेन्जर　642. *—Passenger—*

643. Is the train on time?　क्या गाड़ी ठीक समय पर है?　643. *Kyā gāṛī thīk samay par hai?*

644. On which platform does it arrive?　यह किस प्लेटफार्म पर आती है?　644. *Yah kis platform par atī hai?*

645.	On which platform does it stand?	यह किस प्लेटफार्म पर खड़ी होती है ?	*Yah kis platfarm par kharī hoti hai?*
646.	Where can I get a platform ticket?	मुझे प्लेटफार्म टिकट कहां मिलेगा ?	*Mujhe platfarm ticket kahan milegā?*
647.	Which is the booking office?	टिकट मिलने की जगह कहाँ है ?	*Ticket milne kī jagah kahan hai?*
648.	Where is the entrance?	अन्दर जाने का रास्ता कहाँ है ?	*Andar jāne kā rāsta kahan hai?*
649.	Where is the exit?.	बाहर जाने का रास्ता कहाँ है ?	*Bāhar jane kā rastā kahan hai?*
650.	Where can I get a coolie (porter)?	मुझे कूली कहाँ मिलेगा ?	*Mujhe kulī kahan milegā?*
651.	My luggage is heavy.	मेरा सामान भारी है।	*Merā sāmān bhārī hai*

187

652.	How much luggage do they allow free?	कितने सामान का महसूल नहीं लगता ?	Kitne sāmān kā mahsūl nahīn lagatā?
653.	On a third class ticket.	तीसरे दर्जे के टिकट पर।	Tīsara darje ke ticket par
654.	On second class ticket.	दूसरे—	—Dusare—
655.	On first class ticket.	पहले—	—Pahale—
656.	Where can I have it weighed?	यह कहाँ तुलेगा ?	Yah kahan tulegā?
657.	How much do I pay the porter?	मैं कुली को क्या दूँ ?	Main kulī ko kyā dun?
658.	I want a return ticket.	मैं एक जाने का और वापिस आने का टिकट चाहता हूँ।	Main ek jāne ka aur vāpis āne ka ticket chāhatā hun

659.	Which day you want to return?	आप किस दिन लौटना चाहते है?	*Āp kis din lautnā chāhate hain?*
660.	Please leave open date for return journey.	कृपया लौटने की तारीख खुली रहने दीजिये।	*Kripayā lautne ki tārikh khulī rahame dījiye*
661.	We need two seats.	हमें दो सीट चाहिये।	*Hamen do sīt chahiye*
662.	On what days and on what hours to the planes leave?	किस किस दिन और कै कै बजे हवाई जहाज जाते है?	*Kis kis din aur kai kai baje havāī jahaz jāte hain?*
663.	There is a daily service.	हवाई जहाज हर रोज जाते है।	*Hawai jahāz har roz jāte hain*
664.	There are three services everyday.	हरेक दिन तीन बार जहाज जाता है।	*Harek din tīn bār jahāz jātā hai*

665.	How much do you charge for a child?	बच्चे का क्या किराया लेते हैं?	Bachche kā kyā kirāyā lete hain?
666.	It is a baby in arms.	गोद का बच्चा है।	God kā bachchā hai
667.	For babies we charge one tenth.	छोटे बच्चे के लिये दसवाँ हिस्सा।	Chhote bachche ke liye daswan hissā
668.	How much luggage can we take on one plane ticket?	एक टिकट पर हम कितना सामान हवाई जहाज पर ले जा सकते हैं?	Ek ticket par ham kitnā sāmān hawai jahaz par le jā sakate hain
669.	What is the charge for over-weight?.	अधिक सामान के लिये क्या महसूल है?	Adhik sāmān ke live kyā mahsul hai?
670.	When does the plane take off?.	हवाई जहाज कै बजे रवाना होता है?	Hawai jabāz kai baje rāvanā botā hai?

190

671.	Our plane takes off at twelve thirty.	हमारा हवाई जहाज साढ़े बारह बजे रवाना होता है।	Hāmarā hawāī jahāz sādhe bārah baje rāvanā botā hai
672.	Which is next stop?	अब कहाँ रुकेगा ?	Ab kahan rukegā?
673.	How many seats are there in the plane?	जहाज में कितनी सीट है ?	Jahāz men kitnī sīt bain?
674.	At what altitude are we flying?	हम कितनी ऊँचाई पर उड़ रहे हैं ?	Ham kitnī uchāī par ur rabe bain?
675.	At what speed are we flying?	हम किस गति से उड़ रहे हैं ?	Ham kis gai se ur rabe bain?
676.	Is is necessary to get inoculated before travel?	क्या यात्रा से पहले टीका लगवाना जरूरी है ?	Kyā yātrā se pahale tīkā lagvānā jarurī hai?
677.	When do we arrive?	हम कब पहुँचेंगे ?	Ham kab pahunchenge?

191

678.	Flying gives me nausea.	उड़ने में मेरा जी मचलाता है।	678.	*Urane se merā jī machlātā hai.*
679.	I like flying.	उड़ने में मुझे अच्छा लगता है।	679.	*Urane men mujhe achchhā lāgatā hai*
680.	Which town is below us?	नीचे कौन सा शहर है?	680.	*Nīche kaun sā shahar hai?*
681.	Which mountain is below us?	—सा पहाड़—	681.	*—Sā pahāṛ—*
682.	Which river is below us?	—सी नदी—	682.	*—Sī nadi—*
683.	Which place is below us.	—सी जगह—	683.	*—Sī jagah—*
684.	How may hours does our flight take?	हमारी हवाई यात्रा में कितना समय लगेगा?	684.	*Hāmarī hāwai yātrā men kitnā samay lagegā?*
685.	Is it necessary to go to the customs counter?	क्या कस्टम की जांच के लिये जाना जरूरी है?	685.	*Kyā kastam kī janch ke liye jānā jarurī hai?*

686.	I have nothing to declare.	मेरे पास कोई महसूली चीज नहीं है।	Mere pās koī mahsuli chīj nahīn hai
687.	Still, you must go.	फिर भी आप को जाना चाहिये।	Phir bhā āp ko jānā chāhiye
688.	Checking is necessary.	जाँच जरूरी है।	Janch jaruri hai
689.	Our plane is running late.	हमारा जहाज लेट चल रहा है।	Hāmarā jahāz let chal rahā hai
690.	I hope there is no engine trouble.	मैं आशा करता हूँ कि इंजिन में कोई गड़बड़ नहीं है।	Main ashā kartā hun ki ingin men koi garbar nahīn hai
691.	We have arrived on time.	हम समय पर आ पहुँचे।	Ham samay par ā pahunche

193

Chapter 34

Syntax

Introduction

This part deals with grammar. It is not possible to provide complete instruction on grammar of any language in few pages. The aim here is to acquaint the readers with a brief outline touching the salient features. A child is not taught grammar but becomess so proficient in his mother tongue at the age of five, that another person who has not picked up the language by direct method cannot compete with the former even at the age of sixteen.

The entire subject, dealt with in this part has for facility of reference been divided into paras as give below:

SYNTAX

In Hindi the syntax is different from that of English.

In English the syntax is as follows :

I am going to the garden in the evening.

Here we have the subject, then the verb, then the preposition followed by the object. The words expressing time come in the ned. In Hindi the sentence would run as follows :

मैं शाम को बाग जा रहा हूँ।

Main shām kō bāg jā rahā hūn

The subject is followed by sham ko and the verb comes last.

In interrogative sentences, in Hindi, the words how, when, why come after the subject and not in the beginning.

How will you go?	आप कैसे जायेंगे ?
	Āp kaise jāyenge?
What will you eat?	आप क्या खायेंगे ?
	Āp kya khāyenge?

But the sentence 'Will you eat?' would be translated.

Kya ap khayenge?

As regards syntax the points of similarity between English and Hindi are as follows :

(i) The subject (noun or pronoun) as the case may be comes first.

(ii) The adjevtive precedes the noun qualified.

(iii) The conjuction in Hindi is put at the the place as in English.

(iv) Interjections in Hindi also occupy the initial place as in English.

The points of difference are as follows :

(i)   The preposition which precedes the noun (object) in English, comes after the noun (object) in Hindi. In other words the in English becomes the past-position in Hindi.

Example :

to me—mujh **ko,** for him—uske **liye, from** the chair—kursi **se, in the** house—makan men

(ii)   There is difference in the placement of the object. In English the order is subject—verb—object. But in Hindi the order is subject—object—verb.

Example :

I see a cow. **Main ek gay dekthta hun.** मैं एक गाय देखता हूँ।

Here the object **gay** comes after the subject and before the verb. This has been explained in an earlier paragraph also, and is being reiterated, to emphasise it further.

(iii)   Another point of difference is that in English, the adverb comes after the verb, but in Hindi the adverb precedes the verb.

Example :

He is eating slowly. वह धीरे-धीरे खा रहा है।

The order is subject—verb—adverb.

In Hindi we say **vaha dhīre dhīre khā rahā hai.**

Here the order is subject—adverb—verb.

A large number of sentences—as examples have been given in earlier chapters and a number of ready made sentences have been provided in a subsequent part. The use of these sentences would further strengthen the sense of the syntax.

Nouns

संज्ञा (Sangya)

The most important parts of speech are 'nouns' and verbs. We begin with nouns.

There are only two genders in Hindi: masculine (puling पुलिंग) and feminine (striling स्त्रीलिंग). Gender is either based on sex (in the case of human beings and animals) or on usage. There are no hard and fast rules. According to the general rule, all words ending with the vowel i are feminine. Words ending in consonant may be masculine or feminine. But there are many exceptions to the rule which you will learn as you go on. It may be pointed out here the gender is the weakest point of Hindi grammar. This should not discourage learners as they should know at the very out set that it will take time in mastering the gender in Hindi. it is because of the arbitrary of the grammar nature which are established more or less by usage. Some examples of common masculine and feminine nouns are given at the end.

Rules to remember

1. When there is a suffix to a noun which is the subject, the form of the verb changes not according to the subject, but according to the gender and number of the object.

2. When there is no suffix to the noun which is the subject, the form of the verb changes according to the subject.

3. If a masculine noun ends in **a.** the ending changes into **e** when there is a suffix.

4. If a masculine noun ends in **e** in the plural form the ending changes into **on** when there is suffix to it.

5. Feminine noun in the singular number does not change its form even when there is a suffix.

6. Feminine noun in the plural form having **yan** ending, changes into **yon** ending if there is a suffix.

7. Feminine nouns ending in a consonant or any other vowel in a consonant or any other vowel in the plural, into **on** ending if there is a suffix.

Case

When suffixes are used they are the following in different cases.

(i)	Nominative	कर्त्ता ने
(ii)	Objective	कर्म को
(iii)	Instrumental	करण से
(iv)	Dative	सम्प्रदान के लिये, के वास्ते
(v)	Ablative	अपादार से
(vi)	Genitive or possessive	अधिकरण का,की,के
(vii)	Cocative	सम्बोधन से,पर

Examples :

(i)   मोहन ने मिठाई खाई।

(ii) मोहन को किताब दो।

(iii) बस से जाओ।

(iv) मोहन के लिए फल लाओ।

(v)   पेड़ से फल गिरता है।

(vi) पंकज की पेंट अच्छी हैं।

(vii) दुकान मे किताब हैं।

Chapter 35

Pronouns

सर्वनाम (Sarvanam)

A Word that is used instead of a noun is called a pronoun, e.g. I, you, he she,

वह शब्द जोकि संज्ञा के स्थान पर प्रयोग होता है सर्वनाम कहलता है, जैसे मैं, तुम, वह, वह (स्त्रीलिंग)

The use of pronoun in Hindi is more or less the same as in English.

First Person

I	मैं	main
To me	मुझको	mujhkō
My	मेरा	(m) merā
	मेरी	(f) merī
We	हम	ham
To us	हमको	ham kō
Our	हमारा	(m) hamārā
	हमारी	(f) hamārī

Second Person

You	तुम	tum
	आप	āp
To You	तुम को	tumkō
	आपको	āpkō
Your	तुम्हारा	tumhārā (m)
	तुम्हारी	tumhārī (f)
(respectful)	आपका	apkā (m)
	आपकी	apkī (f)

Third Person

He	वह	vah
	वे	vē
She	वह	vah
	वे	vē
It	यह	yah
To him	उसको	uskō
	उनको	unkō
To her	उसको	uskō
	उनको	unkō

To it	इसको	iskō
They	वे	vē
To them	उनको	unkō
Their	उनका	(m) unkā
	उनकी	(f) unkī

Demonstrative Relative etc.

This	यह	yah
That	वह	vah
These	ये	yē
Those	वे	vē
Who?	कौन ?	kaūn
Whom?	किसको ?	kisko
	किनको ?	kinko

Chapter 36

Adjectives

विशेषण (Visheshan)

An adjective qualifies or adds something to the meaning of a noun or a pronoun.

जिस पद से संज्ञा या सर्वनाम की विशेषता (गुण, दोष, सर्ख्या, परिमाण आदि) का बोध हो उसे विशेषण कहते हैं

Kinds of Adjectives

विशेषण के भेद

1. गुणवाचक विशेषण (Adjectives of Quality)
2. परिमाणवाचक विशेषण (Adjectives of Qauntity)
3. संख्यावाचक विशेषण (Numeral Adjective)
4. सार्वनामिक विशेषण (Demonstrative Adjective)

यह गोरा लडका है।	yah gōrā larkā hai	This boy is fair.
यह गोरी लडकी हैं।	yah gōrī larkī hai	This girl is fair.

1. If an adjective ends with **a** sound, it declines according to the number and gender of the noun it qualifies. In the first set of sentences above, the noun **larka** and the qualifying adjective **gora** both have **a** ending and decline.

यह बड़ा घर है।	yah barā ghar hai.
यह बड़ी मेज़ है।	yah barī mēz hai.

2.   In the above sentences, while the adjective **bara** ends in **a** the nouns **ghar** and **mez** end in a consonant. But the adjective declines as it does in the above sentences. The second rule to remember, therefore, is: **an adjective ending in a sound will change its ending according to the number and gender of the noun it qualifies even if the noun does not end in a sound.**

There are some adjectives which do not change form with change in number or gender. For example.

अमीर	amīr	rich
गरीब	garīb	poor
जवान	jawān	young
ख़राब	kharāb	bad, poor in quality
ख़ूबसूरत	khubsūrat	beautiful
बढ़िया	badhiyā	excellent, high quality
ईमानदार	imāndār	honest
बेईमान	beīmān	dishonest
सुस्त	sūst	dull
तेज	tēj	sharp
चालाक	chālāk	cunning

Chapter 37
Verbs
क्रिया (Kriya)

Ther verb expresses the action or sometimes merely the fact of existence in relation to the subject.

जिस पद से किसी कार्य का करना या होना जाना जाए यह क्रिया कहलाती है

Kinds of Verb

क्रिया के भेद

1. सकर्मक क्रिया (Transitive verb)

2. अकर्मक क्रिया (Intransitive verb)

The verb is the most important part of setence grammatically speaking. If you have mastered the verb you have mastered the language. Here we shall explain the basic forms of the verb without giving the tongue-twisting names of its various forms.

As in English, there are three tenses **(kal)** in Hindi too—Present, Future and Past—**vartman, bhavishya** and **bhut.**

The auxiliary verbs, whcih hav already been introduced in previous chapters, are given here again for not only refreshing your memory but for memorising them.

They are extremely important.

हूँ	hun	an
है	hai	is
हैं	hain	are
था, थी	thā, thī	was
थे, थीं	thē, thīn	were
गा, गी, गे	gā, gī, gē	will shall

As already explained earlier, the **verb always comes last in a sentence and the auxiliary verb comes at the very end. In an interrogative** sentence **the verb does not change its place.** The interrogation is indicated by the tone of the speech. For example.

आपका नाम राम है।

Your name is Ram.

apkā nām Rām hai

आपका नाम राम है?

Your name is Ram.

apkā nām Rām hai?

Sometimes a question may be emphasised by adding **kya** (what) at the beginning.

क्या आपका नाम राम है?

Is your name Ram?

Kyā apkā nām Rām hai?

It is advisable to read aloud this table to understand clearly and to memorize the rules by which the form of a verb is changed. A list of verbs of common usage is given below. The readers are advised to take a few words and form sentences based on the examples given here. But the most important thing is to use what you learn. If you commit mistakes, which you will in the early stages, they will get corrected in the process and you will be able to express yourself clearly and confidently. The first thing one must give up while learning a language is inhibition.

Chapter 38

Adverbs

क्रिया विशेषण (Kriya Visheshan)

An adverb is a word which modifies or adds to the meaning of a verb, an adjective, a preposition or a conjuction or an entire assertive sentence in which case the adverb must stand first in the sentence.

क्रिया-विशेषण यह शब्द है जो क्रिया, विशेषण, सम्बन्ध बोधक, समुच्चय बोधक के अर्थ में विशेषता प्रकट करते है।

Kinds of Adverb

क्रिया-विशेषण के भेद

1. काल वाचक (Adverb of Time)
2. स्थान वाचक (Adverb of Place)
3. परिमाण वाचक (Adverb of Quantity)
4. रीति वाचक (Adverb of Manner)

In the following sentences, it will be observed that adverb precedes an adjective but occupies post position when qualifying a verb. Al adverbs of time and place normally come after the verb. In interrogative sentences, however sometimes adverbs come before the verb:

Some exampples are given below :

1. चाय बहुत गर्म है।   Tea is very hot   *Chāi bahut garam hai*

2. वह तेज चलता है।   He walks fast   *Vah tej chaltā hai*

3. मुझको बिल्कुल नहीं मालूम।	It is not known to me at all	*Mujhkō bilkuk nahīn mālum*
4. मैं वहां जा रहा हूँ।	I am going there	*Main vahan jā rahā hun*
5. वह काफी दूर चला गया	He was gone quite far away	*Vah kafi dur chala gaya*
6. जल्दी जल्दी काम करो	Work fast	*Jaldi jaldi kōm kargayō*
7. आप कहां-कहां जाएंगे?	Which are the places you will go to?	*Āp kahan kahan jāyenge?*
8. घर के आस-पास दुकानें हैं	There are shops near about the house	*Ghar ke aās-pās dukāne hain*
9. मेरा दफ्तर घर से दूर है।	My office is far away from the house	*Merā daftar ghar se dur hai*
10. वह वहां गया।	He went there	*Vha vahān gayā*

In Hindi, adverb whether of time or place or qualifying adjectives or verbs precede in syntax.

Chapter 39

Prepositions

सम्बन्ध बोधक (Sambandh-bodhak)

A preposition is a word placed before a noun or a pronoun to show its relation to something else in the sentence.

जिन अव्यय शब्दों से संज्ञा या सर्वनाम का सम्बन्ध वाक्य के दूसरे शब्दों से जाना जाता है उन्हें सम्बन्ध बोधक अव्यय कहते है।

A preposition, as already explained, is actually a post position in Hindi as it occurs not before but **after** a noun or pronoun. For example **on the table** would be **table on** and **in the room** would be **room in. The book is on the table** would be **the book table on is** (kitabl mez par hai) किताब मेज पर है।

Preposition in Hindi are suffixes to pronouns, but they are written as a separate with nouns.

Rām Ko	but	mujhkō (to me)
राम को		मुझको
mēz par	but	uspar (on that)
मेज पर		उसपर
kamare men	but	usmen
		(on that)
कमरे में		उसमें

Chapter 40
Conjuctions
समुच्चय बोधक (Samuchchaya-bodhak)

A conjuction is a word which joins two words, pharses, clauses or sentences; as— and, but, because etc.

दो शब्दों, वाक्यांशों या वाक्यों को एक क्रिया आदि से मिलाने वाले अव्यय समुच्चय-बोधक कहलाते है, जैसे- और, लेकिन, क्योंकि आदि

The conjuction are, in Hindi as in English; 'links' between two words or two clauses in a sentences.

Example

1. पुनीत कुमार और रवि कुमार।	Punit kumar and Ravi kumar
2. आप जा रहे हैं पर भीग जायेंगं।	You are going but you would get wet.
3. मैं रूपये की परवाह नहीं करता लेकिन देना अच्छी दीजिये।	I do not care for price **but** give me good stuff.

Some conjuctions are used in pairs and are called co-relative conjuctions; as, either....or; neither...nor; ont only...but also; both...and; although (or though)...yet.

Some compound expressions are used are conjuctions and these are compound conjunctions; as, as well as; on condition that; in order that; as soon as.

PART V

Chapter 41
Active Voice

Active voice is in the general use. Therefore, we will explain first of all about active voice. It is frequently used. Here we will explain it with its Hindi equivalents. Passive voice is nt so frequently used. We will explain about it further. In these examples we are are using the verb 'come'.

PRESENT INDEFINITE

Singular

I. First person singular number

(a)	I come	मैं आता हूँ।	*Main ātā hun* (m)
(b)	I come	मैं आती हूँ।	*Main ātī hun* (f)

II. Second person singular number

(a)	You come	तुम आते हो।	*Tum āte ho* (m)
(b)	You come	तुम आती हो।	*Tum ātī ho* (f)

In respectful manner

(a) You come   आप आते हो।   *Āp āe ho*   *(m)*

(b) You come   आप आती हो।   *Āp ati ho*   *(f)*

III. Third person singular number

(a) He comes   वह आता है।   *Wah āābun*   *(m)*

(b) She comes   वह आती है।   *Wah āībun*   *(f)*

In respectful manner

   वे आता है।   *Ve āābai*   *(m)*

   वे आती है।   *Ve āībain*   *(f)*

Plural

I.	We come	हम आते हैं।	Ham āe bain	(m)
		हम आती हैं।	Ham āīhain	(f)
II.	You come	तुम आते हो।	Tum āe bo	(f)
		तुम आती हो।	Tum āībo	(f)
In respectful manner				
		आप आते हैं।	Āp āe bain	(m)
		आप आती हैं।	Āp āīhain	(f)
III.	They come	वे आते हैं।	Ve āe bain	(m)
	—do—	वे आती हैं।	Ve āībain	(f)

215

PRESENT CONTINUOUS

Singular

I. I am coming	मैं आ रहा हूँ।	Main ārabāhun (m)
	मैं आ रही हूँ।	Main ārabāhun (f)
II. You are coming	तुम आ रहे हो।	Tum ārabe ho (f)
—do—	तुम आ रही हो।	Tum ārahīho (f)
In respectful form		
—do—	आप आ रहे हैं।	Āp ārabe hain (m)
—do—	आप आ रहे हैं।	Āp ārahi hain (f)
He is coming	वह आ रहा है।	Vab ārabāhai (m)
She is coming	वह आ रही है।	Vab ārahīhai (f)

216

In respectful form

	वे आ रहे हैं।	*Ve ā̄rabe bain* (m)
	वे आ रही हैं।	*Ve ā̄rabī̄hain* (f)

Plural

I. We are coming

	हम आ रहे हैं।	*Ham ā̄rabe bain* (m)
	हम आ रही रही है।	*Ham ā̄rabī̄hain* (f)

II. You are coming

	तुम आ रहे हो।	*Tum ā̄rabe bo* (f)
	तुम आ रही हो।	*Tum ā̄rabī̄ho* (f)

In respectful manner

III. They are coming

	आप आ रहे हैं।	*Ap ā̄rabe bain* (m)
	आप आ रही हैं।	*Āp ā̄rabi bain* (f)
	वे आ रहे हैं।	*Ve ā̄rabe bain* (m)
	वे आ रही हैं।	*Ve ā̄rabī̄hain* (f)

PRESENT PERFECT

Singular

I. I have come	मैं आया हूँ।	Main āyā hun	(m)
	मैं आयी हूँ।	Main āyī hun	(f)
II. You have been coming	तुम आये हो।	Tum āye ho	(f)
	तुम आयी हो।	Tum āyī ho	(f)
In respectful manner			
	आप आये हैं।	Āp āye hain	(m)
	आप आयी हैं।	Āp āyī hain	(f)
III. He has come	वे आया है।	Vah āyā hai	(m)
She has come	वे आयी है।	Vah āyī hai	(f)

In respectful manner

| | | वे आये हैं। | Ve āye hain | (m) |
| | | वे आयी हैं। | Ve āyi hain | (f) |

Plural

I. We have been coming	हम आये हैं।	Ham āye hain	(m)
	हम आयी हैं।	Ham āyi hain	(f)
II. You have been coming	तुम आये हो।	Tum āye bo	(f)
	तुम आयी हो।	Tum āyi ho	(f)

In respectful form

III. They have come	आप आये हैं।	Āp āye hain	(m)
	आप आयी हैं।	Ap āyi hain	(f)
	वे आये हैं।	Ve āye hain	(m)
	वे आयी हैं।	Ve āyi hain	(f)

PRESENT PERFECT CONTINUOUS

Singular

I. I have been coming	मैं आता रहा हूँ।	*Main ā́arabā́bun*	*(m)*
	मैं आती रही हूँ।	*Main ā́i rabī́bun*	*(f)*
II. You have been coming	तुम आते रहे हो।	*Tum ā́e rabe bo*	*(f)*
	तुम आती रही हो।	*Tum ā́i rabi bo*	*(f)*

In respectful manner

	आप आते रहे हैं।	*Āp ā́e rabe bain*	*(m)*
	आप आती रही हैं।	*Āp ā́i rabī́bain*	*(f)*
III. He has been coming	वह आता रहा है।	*Wab ā́a rabā́bai*	*(m)*
She has been coming	वह आती रही है।	*Wab ā́i rabī́bai*	*(f)*

220

In respectful manner

वे आते रहे हैं।   *Ve ate rabe hain* (m)
वे आती रही हैं।   *Ve āīrabīhain* (f)

Plural

I. We have been coming   हम आते रहे हैं।   *Ham āe rabe hain* (m)
  हम आती रही हैं।   *Ham āīrabi bain* (f)

II. You have been coming   तुम आते रहे हो।   *Tum āe rabe b* (f)
  तुम आती रही हो।   *Tum āīrabī bo* (f)

In respectful form

III. They have been coming   आप आते रहे हैं।   *Āp āe rabe hain* (m)
  आप आती रही हैं।   *Āp āīrabi hain* (f)
  वे आते रहे हैं।   *Ve āe rabe hain* (m)
  वे आती रही हैं।   *Ve āīrabī hain* (f)

221

PAST INDEFINITE

Singular

I. I came	मैं आया।	Main āyā	(m)
	मैं आयी।	Main āyī	(f)
II. You came	तुम आये।	Tum āye	(f)
	तुम आयीं।	Tum āyī	(f)
In respectful form	आप आये।	Āp aye	(m)
	आप आयीं।	Āp āyī	(f)
III. He came	वह आया।	Veb āyā	(m)
She came	वह आयी।	Veb āyī	(f)

222

In respectful form

वे आये।	Ve āye	(m)
वे आयीं।	Ve āyī̄	(f)

Plural

I. We come

हम आये।	Ham āye	(m)
हम आयीं।	Ham āyī̄	(f)

II. You come

तुम आये।	Tum āye	(m)
तुम आयीं।	Tum āyī̄	(f)

In respectful form

आप आये।	Āp āye	(m)
आप आयीं।	Āp āyī̄	(f)

III. They came

वे आये।	Ve āye	(m)
वे आयीं।	Ve āyī̄	(f)

PAST CONTINUOUS

Singular

I. I was coming	मैं आ रहा था।	*Main a raha tha*	*(m)*
	मैं आ रही था।	*Main a rahi thi*	*(m)*
II. You were coming	तुम आ रहे थी।	*Tum a rahe the*	*(f)*
	तुम आ रही थी।	*Tum a rahi thi*	*(f)*
In respectful form			
	आप आ रहे थे।	*Ap a rahe the*	*(m)*
	आप आ रही थीं।	*Ap a rahi thin*	*(f)*
III. He was coming	वह आ रहा था।	*Veh a raha tha*	*(m)*
She was coming	वह आ रही थी।	*Veh a rahi thi*	*(f)*

224

Plural

I.	We were coming	हम आ रहे थे।	*Ham a rāhe the* (m)
		हम आ रही थीं।	*Ham ārahīthī̃* (m)
II.	You were coming	तुम आ रहे थे।	*Tum ārhe the* (f)
		तुम आ रही थीं।	*Tum ārahīthin* (m)

In respectful manner

		आप आ रहे थे।	*Āp ārahe the* (m)
		आप आ रही थीं।	*Āp ārahīthin* (f)
III.	They were coming	वे आ रहे थे।	*Ve ārahe the* (m)
		वे आ रही थीं।	*Ve ārabīthin* (f)

225

PAST PERFECT

Singular

I. I had come	मैं आया था।	*Main āyā thā*	(m)
	मैं आयी थी।	*Main āyī thī*	(m)
II. You had come	तुम आये थे।	*Tum āye the*	(f)
	तुम आई थीं।	*Main āyī thī*	(f)
In respectful manner			
	आप आये थे।	*Āp āye the*	(m)
	आप आयी थीं।	*Āp āyī thī*	(f)
III. He had come	वह आया था।	*Veh āyā thā*	(m)
She had come	वह आयी थी।	*Veh āyī thī*	(f)

226

In respectful manner

वे आये थे।	*Ve āye the*	(m)
वे आयी थीं।	*Ve āyīthīṁ*	(f)

Plural

I. We had come

हम आये थे।	*Ham āye the*	(m)
हम आयी थीं।	*Ham āyīthīṁ*	(m)

II. You had come

तुम आये थे।	*Tum āye the*	(f)
तुम आयी थीं।	*Tum āyī tbīṁ*	(m)

In respectful manner

III. They had come

आप आये थे।	*Āp āye the*	(m)
आप आयीं थीं।	*Āp āyṁ tbīṁ*	(f)
वे आये थे।	*Ve āye the*	(m)
वे आयी थीं।	*Ve āyīthīṁ*	(f)

PAST PERFECT CONTINUOUS

Singular

I. I had been coming	मैं आता रहा था।	*Main ā̄rabā̄tbā̄(m)*
	मैं आती रही थी।	*Main āi rabi thi (m)*
II. You had been coming	तुम आते रहे थे।	*Tum āte rahe the (f)*
	तुम आती रही थी।	*Tum ā̄ī rabī̄ tbī̄ (f)*

Respectful of the above

	आप आते रहे थे।	*Āp āe rahe the (m)*
	आप आती रही थी।	*Āp ā̄rabī̄tbm̄ (f)*
III. He had been coming	वह आता रहा था।	*Veh ā̄rabā̄tbā (m)*
She had been coming	वह आती रही थी।	*Veh ā̄rrabī̄tbī̄ (f)*

228

Respect of the above

वे आते रहे थे।   Ve āte rahe the (m)

वे आती रही थीं।   Ve ā̃ī rahī thī̃ (f)

Plural

I. We had been coming   हम आते रहे थे   Ham āte rab the (m)

हम आती रही थीं   Ham ā̃ī rahī tbhī̃ (m)

II. You had been coming   तुम आते रहे थे   Tum āte rabe the (f)

तुम आती रही थीं   Tum ā̃ī rabī tbhī̃ (m)

Respectful of the above

III. They had been coming   आप आते रहे थे   Ap āte rabe the (m)

आप आती रही थीं   Ap ā̃ī rabī tbhī̃ (f)

वे आते रहे थे   Ve āte rabe the (m)

वे आती रही थीं   Ve ā̃ī rahī tbhī̃ (f)

CONDITIONAL PAST PERFECT

Singular

I. If I had come	अगर मैं आता।	Agar main ātā	(m)
	अगर मैं आती।	Agar main ātī	(m)
If we had come	अगर हम आते।	Agar ham āte	(f)
	अगर हम आतीं।	Agar ham ātīṁ	(m)
II. If you had come	अगर तुम आते।	Agar tum āte	(f)
	अगर तुम आतीं।	Agar tum ātīṁ	(f)
In respectful manner			
	अगर आप आते।	Agar āp āte	(m)
	अगर आप आतीं।	Agar āp ātīṁ	(f)

III. If he had come   अगर वह आता।   *Agar veh ātā*   *(m)*
    If she had come   अगर वे आती।   *Agar veh ātī*   *(f)*

In respectful manner

   अगर वे आते।   *Agar ve āte*   *(m)*
   अगर वे आतीं।   *Agar ve ātīṁ*   *(f)*

FUTURE INDEFINITE
Singular

I. I will come	मैं आऊंगा	*Main aūṅgā*	*(m)*
	मैं आऊंगी	*Main aūṅgī*	*(m)*
II. You will come	तुम आओगे	*Tum āoge*	*(f)*
	तुम आओगी	*Tum āogī*	*(f)*
Respectful of the above			
	आप आयेंगे	*Āp ayenge*	*(m)*
	आप आयेंगी	*Āp āyengī*	*(f)*
III. He will come	वह आयेगा	*Veh āyegā*	*(m)*
She will come	वह आयेगी	*Veh āyegī*	*(f)*
Respectful of the above			
	वे आयेंगे	*Ve āyenge*	*(m)*
	वे आयेंगी	*Ve āyengī*	*(f)*

232

Plural

I. We will come	हम आयेंगे।	Ham āyenge	(m)
	हम आयेंगी।	Ham āyengī	(m)
II. You will come	तुम आओगे।	Tum āoge	(f)
	तुम आओगी।	Tum āogī	(m)

Respectful of the above

III. They will come	आप आयेंगे।	Āp āyenge	(m)
	आप आयेंगी।	Āp āyengī	(f)
	वे आयेंगे।	Ve āyenge	(m)
	वे आयेंगी।	Ve āyengī	(f)

FUTURE CONTINUOUS

Singular

I. I will be coming	मैं आता रहूंगा।	*Main āā rahungā(m)*
	मैं आती रहूंगी।	*Main āī rahungī (m)*
II. You will be coming	तुम आते रहोगे।	*Tum ate raboge (f)*
	तुम आती रहोगी।	*Tum āī rabogī (f)*

Respectful of the above

	आप आते रहेंगे।	*Āp ate rabenge (m)*
	आप आती रहेंगी।	*Āp āī rabengī (f)*
III. He will be coming	वह आता रहेगा।	*Veh āā rabegā (m)*
She will be coming	वे आती रहेंगी।	*Veh āī rabegī (f)*

Plural

I. We will be coming	हम आते रहेंगे।		*Ham āte rahenge (m)*
	हम आती रहेंगी।		*Ham ātī rahengī (m)*
II. You will be coming	तुम आते रहोगे।		*Tum āte rahoge (f)*
	तुम आती रहोगी।		*Tum ātī rahogī (m)*

Respectful of the above

आप आते रहेंगे		*Āp āte rahenge (m)*
आप आती रहेंगी।		*Āp ātī rahengi (f)*

FUTURE PERFECT

Singular

I. I shall have come	मैं आ चुका होऊंगा।	*Main ā chukā boungā (m)*	
	मैं आ चुकी होऊंगी।	*Main ā chukī houngī (m)*	
II. You will have come	तुम आ चुके होगे।	*Tum ā chuke boge*	(f)
	तुम आ चुकी होगी।	*Tum ā chukī hogi (f)*	
Respectful of the above			
	आप आ चुके होंगे।	*Āp ā chuke bonge (m)*	
	आप आ चुकी होंगी।	*Āp ā chukī bongī (f)*	
III. He will have come	वह आ चुका होगा।	*Veh a chukā bogā (m)*	
She will have come	वह आ चुकी होगी।	*Veh ā chukī hogī (f)*	
In respectful manner			
	वे आ चुके होंगे।	*Ve ā chuke bonge (m)*	
	वे आ चुकी होंगी।	*Ve ā chukī bongī (f)*	

236

Regarding the perfection of any particular action above form of sentences is used. Otherwise the below given form is used.

Singular

I. I have come	मैं आ गया हूँ।	*Main āgayā̄bun (m)*
	मैं आ गई हूँ।	*Main āgayī̄bun (m)*
II. You have come	तुम आ गये हो।	*Tum āgaye bo (f)*
	तुम आ गई हो।	*Tum āgayi bo (f)*

Respectful of the above

	आप आ गये हैं।	*Āp āgaye bain (m)*
	आप आ गयी हैं।	*Āp āgayī̄bain (f)*
III. He has come	वह आ गया है।	*Vea āgayā̄hai (m)*
She has come	वह आ गई है।	*Veb āgayī̄hai (f)*

237

Respectful of the above

वे आ गये हैं। Ve ā gaye hain (m)
वे आ गई हैं। Ve ā gayī hain (f)

Plural

I. We come हम आ गए हैं। Ham ā gaye hain (m)
हम आ गई हैं। Ham ā gayī hain (f)

II. You have come तुम आ गये हो। Tum ā gaye ho (f)
तुम आ गई हो। Tum ā gayī ho (f)

III. They have come वे आ गये हैं। Ve ā gaye hain (f)
वे आ गई हैं। Ve ā gayī hain (f)

FUTURE PERFECT CONTINUOUS

Singular

I. I shall have been coming	मैं आता रहा हूंगा।	Main ātā rahā bungā	(m)
	मैं आती रही हूँगी।	Main ātī rahī bungī	(f)
II. You will have been coming	तुम आते रहे होगे।	Tum āte rahe hoge	(f)
	तुम आती रही होगी।	Tum ātī rahī hogī	(f)
Respectful of the above			
	आप आते रहे होंगे।	Āp āte rahe hoonge	(m)
	आप आती रही होंगी।	Āp ātī rahī hongī	(f)
III. He will have been coming	वह आता रहा होगा।	Veb ātā rahā hogā	(m)
She will have been coming	वह आती रही होगी।	Veb ātī rahī hogī	(f)

239

Plural

I. We shall have been coming	हम आते रहे होंगे।	*Ham āte rahe bonge*	(m)
	हम आती रही होंगी।	*Ham āīrabīhongi*	(f)
II. You will have been coming	तुम आते रहे होंगे।	*Tum āte rahe bonge*	(f)
	तुम आते रहे होंगी।	*Tum āīrabi bongī*	(f)
Respectful of the above	आप आते रहे होंगे।	*Ap āte rahe bonge*	(m)
	आप आती रही होंगी।	*Ap āīrabībongī*	(f)
III. They will have been coming	वे आते रहे होंगे।	*Ve āte rahe bonge*	(m)
	वे आती रही होंगी।	*Ve āīrabībongī*	(m)
Respectful of the above	वे आते रहे होंगे।	*Ve āte rahe hoonge*	(m)
	वे आती रही होंगी।	*Ve āīrabībongī*	(f)

Chapter 42
Passive Voice

Passive voice is the subject of the use of transitive verb. This voice is not frequently used. We are giving Hindi quivalents in passive voice as well as English. In these examples we are using the words आ पढ़ाना

PRESENT INDEFINITE

Singular

I. I am taught	मैं पढ़ाया जाता हूँ।	Main padhāyā jātā hun	(m)
	मैं पढ़ायी जाती हूँ।	Main padhāyi jāti hun	(f)
II. You are taught	तुम पढ़ाये जाते हो।	Tum pādhāye jāte bo	(f)
	तुम पढ़ायी जाती हो।	Tum padhāyi jāti ho	(f)

241

Respectful of the above

आप पढ़ाये जाते हैं। *Āp pāḍbāye jāte hain* (m)
आप पढ़ायी जाती हैं। *Āp Padbāyī jāī hain* (f)

III. He is taught
वह पढ़ाया जाता है। *Veh padhaya jāā hai* (m)
She is taught
वह पढ़ायी जाती है। *Veh adbāyī jāī hai* (f)

Respectful of the above

वे पढ़ाये जाते हैं। *Ve padbāye jāte hain* (m)
वे पढ़ायी जाती हैं। *Ve padbāyī jāī hain* (f)

Plural

I. We are taught
हम पढ़ाये जाते हैं। *Ham padbāye jāte hain* (m)
हम पढ़ायी जाते हैं। *Ham padbāyī jāī hain* (f)

II. You are taught
तुम पढ़ाये जाते हो। *Tum padbāye jāte ho* (f)
तुम पढ़ायी जाती हो। *Tum padbāyī jāī ho* (f)

242

Respectful of the above

आप पढ़ाये जाते हो।	*Āp padhāye jāte ho*	(m)
आप पढ़ायी जाती हो।	*Āp Padhāyī jātī ho*	(f)

III. They are taught

वे पढ़ाये जाते हैं।	*Ve padhāye jāte hain*	(m)
वे पढ़ायी जाती हैं।	*Ve padhāyī jātī hain*	(m)

PRESENT CONTINUOUS

Singular

I. I am being taught   मैं पढ़ाया जा रहा हूँ।   *Main padhāyā jā rabā bun (m)*

                     मैं पढ़ायी जा रही हूँ।   *Main padhāyī jā rab bun* (f)

II. You are being taught   तुम पढ़ाये जा रहे हो।   *Tum padhāye jā rabe ho* (f)

                     तुम पढ़ायी जा रही हो।   *Tum padhāyī jā rabī bo* (f)

Plural

I. We are being taught   हम पढ़ाये जा रहे हैं।   *Ham padhāye jā rabe hain (m)*

                   हम पढ़ायी जा रही हैं।   *Ham pādbayī jā rabī hain* (f)

II. You are being taught   तुम पढ़ाये जा रहे हो।   *Tum padbāye jā rabe bo* (f)

                     तुम पढ़ायी जा रही हो।   *Tum padbāyī jā rabī ho* (f)

Respectful of the above

	आप पढ़ाये जा रहे हो।	*Āp padbāye ja rabe bo*	*(m)*
	आप पढ़ायी जा रही हो।	*Āp Padbāyī ja rabi bo*	*(f)*
III. They are being taught	वे पढ़ाये जा रहे हैं।	*Ve padbāye jā rabe hain*	*(m)*
	वे पढ़ाई जा रही हैं।	*Ve padbāyī ja rabī hain*	*(m)*

Respectful of the above

	आप पढ़ाये जा रहे हो।	*Āp padbāye jā rabe bo*	*(m)*
	आप पढ़ायी जा रही हो।	*Āp padbāyī jā rabi bo*	*(f)*
III. He is being taught	वह पढ़ाया जा रहा है।	*Veb padbāya jā rabā bai*	*(m)*
She is being taught	वह पढ़ायी जा रही है।	*Veb padbāyī ja rabī bai*	

Respectful of the above

	वे पढ़ाये जा रहे हैं।	*Ve padbāye jā rabe hain*	*(m)*
	वे पढ़ायी जा रही हैं।	*Ve padbāyī ja rabī hain*	*(f)*

PRESENT PERFECT

Singular

I. I have been taught   मैं पढ़ाया जा चुका हूँ।   *Main padhāya jā chukā hun (m)*

मैं पढ़ाया गया हूँ।   *Main padhāyā gayā hun (f)*

मैं पढ़ायी जा चुकी हूँ।   *Main padhāyī ja chīkī hun (f)*

मैं पढ़ायी गयी हूँ।   *Main padhāyī gayī hun(f)*

II. You have been taught   तुम पढ़ाये जा चुके हो।   *Tum padhāye jā chuke ho (f)*

तुम पढ़ाये गये हो।   *Tum padhāye gaye ho (f)*

तुम पढ़ायी जा चुकी हो।   *Tum padhāye jā chukī ho (f)*

तुम पढ़ायी गयी हो।   *Tum padhāyī gayī ho   (f)*

Respectful of the above	आप पढ़ाये जा चुके हो।	*Āp padhāye jā chuke hain (f)*
	आप पढ़ाये जा गये हैं।	*Āp padhāye gaye hain(f)*
	आप पढ़ायी जा चुकी हैं।	*Āp Padhayi jā ch ūke ī (f)*
	आप पढ़ायी गयी हैं।	*Āp padhāyi gayi hain (f)*
III. He has been taught	वह पढ़ाया जा चुका हैं।	*Veh padhāyā jā ch 'kā bai (f)*
	वह पढ़ाया गया हैं।	*Veh padhāyā gayā bai (f)*
She has been taught	वह पढ़ायी जा चुकी हैं।	*Veh padhāyī jā chūke ī hai (f)*
	वह पढ़ायी गयी हैं।	*Veh padhāyī gayī hain (f)*
Respectful of the above	वे पढ़ाये जा चुके हैं।	*Ve padhāye jā chūke hain (f)*
	वे पढ़ाये गये हैं।	*Ve padhāye gaye hain (f)*
	वे पढ़ायी जा चुकी हैं।	*Ve padhāyī ja chūke ī hain (f)*
	वे पढ़ायी गयी हैं।	*Ve padhāyī gayī hain (f)*

Plural

I. We have been taught

हम पढ़ाये जा चुके हैं।		*Ham padhāye jā chuke hain (m)*
हम पढ़ाये गये हैं।		*Ham padhāye gaye main (f)*
हम पढ़ायी जा चुकी हैं।		*Ham padhāyī jā chukī hain (f)*
हम पढ़ायी गयी हैं।		*Hum padhāyī gayī hain (f)*

II. You have been taught

तुम पढ़ाये जा चुके हो।		*Tum padhāye jā chuke ho (m)*
तुम पढ़ाये गये हो।		*Tum padhāye gaye ho (f)*
तुम पढ़ायी जा चुकी हो।		*Tum padhayī ja chukī ho (f)*
तुम पढ़ायी गयी हो।		*Tum padhāyī gayī ho (f)*

Respectful of the above

आप पढ़ाये जा चुके हो।		*Āp padhāye jā chuke ho (f)*
आप पढ़ाये गये हो।		*Āp padhāye gaye hain (f)*
आप पढ़ायी जा चुकी हो।		*Āp padhāyī jā chukī hain (f)*

III. They have been taught वे पढ़ाये जा चुके हैं।   *Ve padhāye jā chuke hain (m)*

वे पढ़ाये गये हैं।   *Ve padhāye gaye hain (m)*

वे पढ़ायी जा चुकी हैं।   *Ve padhāyī jā chukī hain (f)*

वे पढ़ायी गयी हैं।   *Ve padhāyī gayī hain (f)*

Note — In Perfect Continous there is no Passive.

249

PAST INDEFINITE

Singular

I. I was taught	मैं पढ़ाया गया।	Main padhāya gayā	(m)
	मैं पढ़ायी गयी।	Main padhāyī gayī	(f)
II. You were taught	तुम पढ़ाये गये।	Tum padhāye gaye	(f)
	मैं पढ़ायी गयी।	Main padhāyī gayī	(f)

Respectful of the above

	आप पढ़ाये गये।	Āp padhāye gaye	(m)
	आप पढ़ायी गयीं।	Āp padhāyī gāyī	(f)
III. He was taught	वह पढ़ाया गया।	Veh padhāyā gayā	(f)
She was taught	वह पढ़ायी गयी।	Veh padhāyī gayi	(f)

Respectful of the above

| | | वे पढ़ाये गये। | *Ve padhāye gaye* | (m) |
| | | वे पढ़ाई गयीं। | *Ve padhāyī gahī* | (f) |

Plural

I. We were taught	हम पढ़ाये गये।	*Ham padhāye gaye*	(m)
	हम पढ़ाई गयीं।	*Ham padhāyī gayī*	(f)
II. You were taught	तुम पढ़ाये गये।	*Tum padhāye gaye*	(f)
	तुम पढ़ाई गयीं।	*Tum padhāyī gāyī*	(f)

Respectful of the above

III. They were taught	आप पढ़ाये गये।	*Āp padhaye gaye*	(m)
	आप पढ़ाई गयीं।	*Āp padhāyī gayī*	(f)
	वे पढ़ाये गये।	*Ve padhāye gaye*	(m)
	वे पढ़ाई गयीं।	*Ve padhāyī gayī*	(m)

251

PAST CONTINUOUS

Singular

I. I was being taught	मैं पढ़ाया जा रहा था।	*Main paḍhāya jā rabā tbā (m)*
	मैं पढ़ायी जा रही थी।	*Main paḍhāyi jā rabā tbī (f)*
II. You were being taught	तुम पढ़ाये जा रहे थे।	*Tum paḍhāye jā rabe bo (f)*
	तुम पढ़ायी जा रही थी।	*Tum paḍhāyi jā rabi tbī (f)*
Respectful of the above	आप पढ़ाये जा रहे थे।	*Āp paḍhāye jā rabe the (m)*
	आप पढ़ायी जा रही थी।	*Āp paḍhāyi jā rabi tbī (f)*
III. He was being taught	वह पढ़ाया जा रहा था।	*Veb paḍhāya jā rabā tbā (f)*
She was being taught	वह पढ़ायी जा रही थी।	*Veb paḍhāyi jā rabi tbī (f)*
Respectful of the above	वे पढ़ाये जा रहे थे।	*Ve paḍhāye jā rabe the (m)*
	वे पढ़ायी जा रही थी।	*Ve paḍhāyi jā rabi tbī (f)*

Plural

I. We were being taught	हम पढ़ाये जा रहे थे।	Ham padhāye jā rahe the	(m)
	हम पढ़ायी जा रही थीं।	Ham padhāyī jā rahī thīn	(f)
II. You were being taught	तुम पढ़ाये जा रहे थे।	Tum padhāye jā rahe the	(f)
	तुम पढ़ायी जा रही थीं।	Tum padhāyī jā rahī thīn	(f)

Respectful of the above

	आप पढ़ाये जा रहे थे।	Āp padhāye jā rahe the	(m)
	आप पढ़ायी जा रही थीं।	Āp padhāyī jā rahī thīn	(f)
III. They were being taught	वे पढ़ाये जा रहे थे।	Ve padhāye jā rahe the	(m)
	वे पढ़ायी जा रही थीं।	Ve padhāyī jā rahī thī	(m)

253

PAST PERFECT

Singular

I. I had been taught	मैं पढ़ाया गया था।	*Main padbāya gaya tha (m)*
	मैं पढ़ायी गयी थी।	*Main padbāyī gayī thī* (f)
II. You have been taught	तुम पढ़ाये गये थे।	*Tum padbāye gaye the* (f)
	तुम पढ़ायी गयी थी।	*Tum padbāyī gayī thin* (f)
Respectful of the above		
You have been taught	आप पढ़ाये गये थे।	*Āp Padbāye gaye the* (m)
	आप पढ़ायी गयी थी।	*Āp padbāyī gayi thin*
III. He had been taught	वह पढ़ाया गया था।	*Veh padbāya gayā tba* (f)
She had been taught	वह पढ़ायी गयी थी।	*Veh padbāyī gabī thī* (f)
Respectful of the above		
	वे पढ़ाये गये थे।	*Ve pabdāye gaye tba* (m)
	वे पढ़ायी गयी थीं	*Ve padbāyī gayī thī* (f)

254

Plural

I. We had been taught
हम पढ़ाये गये थे।   *Hum padhāye gaye the (m)*
हम पढ़ायी गयी थीं   *Ham padhāyī gayī thīṁ (f)*

II. You had been taught
तुम पढ़ाये गये थे   *Tum padhaye gaye the (f)*
तुम पढ़ायी गयी थीं।   *Tum padhāyī gayī thīṁ (f)*

III. They had been taught
वे पढ़ाये गये थे।   *Ve padhāye gaye the (m)*
वे पढ़ायी गयीं थे।   *Ve padhāyī gayī thīṁ (m)*

FUTURE INDEFINITE

Singular

I. I shall be taught	मैं पढ़ाया जाऊंगा।	*Main padhāya jaūngā* (m)
	मैं पढ़ायी जाऊंगी।	*Main padhāyi jaūngā* (f)
II. You will be taught	तुम पढ़ाये जाओगे।	*Tum padhāye jaoge* (f)
	तुम पढ़ायी जाओगी।	*Tum padhāyi jaogī* (f)
Respectful of the above		
	आप पढ़ाये जावेंगे।	*Āp padhāye jawenge* (m)
	आप पढ़ायी जावेंगी।	*Āp padhāyi jawengī* (f)
III. He will be taught	वह पढ़ाया जावेगा।	*Veh padhāyā jawegā* (m)
She will be taught	वह पढ़ाया जावेगी।	*Veh padhāyi jāwegī* (f)
Respectful of the above		
	वे पढ़ाये जावेंगे।	*Ve padhāye jāwenge* (m)
	वे पढ़ायी जावेंगी।	*Ve padhāyi jāwengī* (f)

256

Plural

I. We shall be taught — हम पढ़ाये जावेंगे।   *Ham padhāye jāwenge* (m)

                      हम पढ़ायी जावेंगी।   *Ham padhāy jāwengā* (f)

II. You will be taught — तुम पढ़ाये जाओगे।   *Tum padhāye jāoge* (f)

                      तुम पढ़ायी जाओगी।   *Tum padhāyī jāogi* (f)

Respectful of the above

                      आप पढ़ाये जावेंगे।   *Āp padhāye jāwenge* (m)

                      आप पढ़ायी जावेंगी।   *Āp padhāyÝ jāwengi* (f)

III. They will be taught — वे पढ़ाये जावेंगे।   *Ve padhāye jāwenge* (m)

                      वे पढ़ायी जावेंगी।   *Ve padhāyī jāwengi* (m)

In future continuous and perfect continuous there is no passive voice.

FUTURE PERFECT

Singular

I. I shall have been taught मैं पढ़ाया जा चुका होऊंगा।

Main padbāya jā cb ūka houngā (m)

मैं पढ़ायी जा चुकी होऊंगी।

Main padbāyī jā chuki boungī (f)

II. You will have been taught तुम पढ़ाये जा चुके होवोगे।

Tum padbāye jā cb ūke bovoge (f)

तुम पढ़ायी जा चुकी होवोगी।

Tum padbayi ja chuki bovogi (f)

Respectful of the above

आप पढ़ाये जा चुके होंगे।

Āp padbāye jā cb ūke bonge (m)

आप पढ़ायी जा चुकी होंगी।

Āp padhayi ja cb ūkī bongī (f)

258

III. He will have been taught वह पढ़ाया जा चुका होगा। *Veh padhāya jā chūka hogā* (f)

  She will have been taught वह पढ़ायी जा चुकी होगी। *Veh padhāyi jā chūki hogi* (f)

Respectful of the above

  वे पढ़ाये जा चुके होवेंगे। *Ve padhāye jā chūke howenge* (m)

  वे पढ़ायी जा चुकी होवेंगी। *Ve padhāyi jā chūki howengi* (f)

Plural

I. We shall have been taught हम पढ़ाये जा चुके होवेंगे। *Ham padhāye jā chūke howenegi* (m)

  हम पढ़ायी जा चुकी होवेंगी। *Ham padhāyi ja chūki hoowengi* (f)

II. You will have been taught तुम पढ़ाये जा चुके होगे।

Tum paḍāaye jā chuke honge (f)

तुम पढ़ायी जा चुकी होगी।

Tum padhbāyī jā chukī hongī (f)

III. They will have been taught वे पढ़ाये जा चुके होवेंगे।

Ve padhbāye jā chuke howenge (m)

वे पढ़ायी जा चुकी होवेंगी।

Ve padhbāye jā chukī howengī (m)

260

PART VI

Chapter 43
Administrative Terms and Important Words

Administrator	प्रशासक	Prashāsak
Advisor	सलाहकार	Salākhār
Agent	अभिकर्ता	Abhikartā
Air Headquarters	वायुसेना मुख्यालय	Vayū sena Mukhyālaya
All India Handicarafts Board	अखिल भारतीय दस्तकारी बोर्ड	Akhil Bhāratīya Dastkārī Bōard
All India Radio	आकाशवाणी	Akāsvanī
Ambassador	राजदूत	Rajdūt
Anti-corruption Branch	भष्टाचार-विरोधी शाखा	Bhrastāchār-virodhī shākha
Appellant	अपीलकर्ता	Apīl kartā
Arbitrator	विवाचक	Vivāchak
Archaeological Department	पुरातत्व विभाग	Purātatva vibhāg
Architect	वास्तुविद्	Vāstuvid
Assessor	निर्धारक	Nirdhārk
Assistant	सहायक	Sahāyak
Attache	सहचारी	Sahachārī
Attendant	परिचर	Parichar
Authority	प्राधिकार, प्राधिकारी, प्राधिकरण	Pradhikār, prādhikārī, prādhikarān
Bacteriologist	जीवाणु-विज्ञानी	jīvanu-vigyānī
Bench	पीठ, कक्ष	Pīth, kaksh
Certain	निश्चित	Nishchit

Certified	प्रमाणित	*Prāmanit*
Citizen	नागरिक	*Nāgrik*
Clergy	पादरी	*Pādarī*
Clause	धारा	*Dhārā*
Colleague	साथी	*Sāthī*
Committee	समिति	*Samiti*
Concur	एकमत होना	*Ekamat honā*
Condone	क्षमा करना	*Kshamā karanā*
Confusion	धबराहट	*Ghabrāhat*
Consent	सहमती	*Sahamatī*
Consider	विचार करना	*Vichār karanā*
Consort	पति या पत्नी	*Pati yā patnī*
Consideration	विचार, आदर	*Vichār, Adār*
Consider	विचार करना	*Vichār karanā*
Conspiracy	षड्यंत्र साजिश	*Saryantra, Sājish*
Constitution	संविधान	*Sanvidhān*
Construction	निर्माण	*Nirmān*
Consult	सलाह लेना	*Salāh lenā*
Consumer	उपभोक्ता	*Upabhōktā*
Contact	सम्पर्क	*Samparak*
Contention	विवाद	*Vivād*
Contempt	अपमान	*Apmān*
Contingency	संभावना	*Sambhāwanā*
Contradict	विरोध करना, बात काटना	*Virōdh karanā, bāt kātnā*
Contrary	विपरित	*Viprit*
Contrast	अन्तर	*Antar*
Control	नियंत्रण	*Niyantrān*
Conversation	बातचीत	*Bātchīt*
Conventional	रिवायती, परंपरागत	*Rivāyatī, parmprāgat*

Conversant	परिचित	*Parichit*
Convey	पहुंचाना, ले जाना	*Pahunchānā, lē jānā*
Convict	अपराधी	*Aprādhi*
Co-operation	साथ देना, सहयोग करना	*Sāth denā, Sahayog karanā*
Correction	सुधार, शोधन	*Sudhār, Shōdhan*
Correspondence	पत्रव्यवहार	*Patravyavhār*
Corruption	भ्रष्टाचार	*Bhrastāchār*
Count	गिनना	*Ginanā*
Country	ग्रामक्षेत्र, देश	*Grām kshetra, Desh*
Couple	विवाहित जोडी	*Vivāhit jorī, yugal*
Course	गति मार्ग	*Gari, Mārg*
Court	अदालत	*Adālat*
Crucial	निर्णायक	*Nirnāyak*
Culture	संस्कृति	*Sanskrit*
Currency	मुद्रा	*Mudrā*
Curve	मोड़	*Mōr*
Custody	हिरासत	*Hirāsat*
Custom	रीति-रिवाज	*Rīti Rivāz*
Dacoity	डाका	*Dākā*
Dagger	छुरा	*Chhurā*
Daily	हर रोज़	*Har rōz*
Damage	हानि	*Hāni*
Danger	खतरा	*Khatrā*
Date	तारीख, खजूर	*Tārikh, khajur*
Deadly	घातक	*Ghātak*
Debar	वंचित करना	*Vanchit karanā*
Debate	वाद-विवाद	*Vād-vivād*
Decade	दशक	*Dashak*
Decent	सभ्य	*Sabhya*

Decide	निश्चय	Nishchay
Declare	घोषणा	Chosnā
Decline	पतन, घट जाना	patan, ghat jana
Dedicate	समर्पण करना	Samarpan, karanā
Defect	कमी,	Kamī,
	छोड़ जाना	Chhor jānā
Defend	रक्षा करना	Rakshā karanā
Defer	स्थागित	Sthāgit
Define	परिभाषा करना	Paribhāshā karanā
Defy	सामना करना	Sāmanā karanā
Degree	उपाधि, डिग्री	Upādhi, digrī
Delegate	प्रतिनिधि	Pritinidhi
Deliver	सौंपना,	Sounpanā
	सुपुर्द करना	Supurd karanā
Deceive	धोखा करना	Dhōkha denā
Demand	मांग	Māng
Delusion	भ्रम	Bhram
Demerits	अवगुण, दोष	Avagun, Dosh
Democracy	गणतंत्र	Ganatantra
Denial	मुकरना,	Mukarnā,
	अस्वीकृति	Aswikriti
Dense	घना	Ghanā
Department	विभाग	Vibhāg
	प्रस्थान	Prasthān, Rāvanā
	रवाना होना	hone
Deposit	जमा करना	Jamā Karanā
Depot	भण्डार, डिपो	Bhandār, Dipo
Deserve	योग्य होना	Yōgya hona
Design	रूपरेखा	Rup-reka
Desire	इच्छा	Ichchhā
Destroy	नष्ट करना	Nast karanā

Detail	विवरण	*Vivaran*
Detect	पता लगाना	*Patā lagānā*
Detective	जासूस	*Jāsus*
Devotion	भक्ति	*Bhakti*
Diet	भोजन, खुराक	*Bhōjan, Khurāk*
Difference	मतभेद	*Matbhed*
Difficult	कठिन	*Kathin*
Director	संचालक	*Senchālak*
Disable	असमर्थ	*Asmarh*
Disappoint	निराश करना	*Nirāsh karanā*
Discipline	अनुशासन	*Anushāsan*
Disclose	ज़ाहिर करना,	*Zāhir karanā,*
	प्रकट करना	*Prakat karanā*
Dismiss	नौकरी से अलग	*Nuakari sē alag*
	कर देना	*kar denā*
Disloyal	बेवफा	*Bevaphā*
Disobey	अवज्ञा	*Avagyā*
Disguise	भेष बदलना	*Bhesh badalanā*
Dispensary	औषधालय	*Aushdhālay*
Display	प्रदर्शन	*Pradarshan*
Distinguish	पहचानना	*Pahachānanā*
Distribute	बटंवारा करना	*Bantavarā karanā*
District	ज़िला	*Zilā*
Disturb	ध्यान बटाना	*Dhyān batānā*
Divide	विभाजित करना	*Vibhājit karanā*
Diverse	विभिन्न	*Vibhinn*
Divorce	तलाक	*Talāk*
Domestic	घरेलू	*Gharelu*
Domicile	स्थायी निवासी	*Sthāyi nivāsi*
Doubt	सन्देह	*Sandeh*
Dowry	दहेज़	*Dahēz*

265

Drink	मद्य-पान, शराब पीना	Madya pān, Sharāb pīnā
Duty	कर्त्तव्य	Karttavya
Early	शीघ्र	Shīghra
Earn	कमाना, अर्जित करना	Kamānā, Arjit karanā
Earnest	सच्चा	Sachchā
Earth	धरती	Dhartī
Easily	आसानी से	Asānī se
East	पूरब	Pūrab
Eccentric	सनकी	Sankī
Economic	आर्थिक	Arthik
Education	शिक्षा	Shikshā
Ego	स्वार्थ भास	Swārth Bhās
Electric	बिजली	Bijalī
Embassy	दूतावास	Dutāvās
Emergency	आपातकाल	Apākāl
Emigrant	उत्प्रवासी	Utpravāsī
Employ	नौकर रखना	Nukar rakhanā
Enclose	बन्द करना	Band karanā
Encash	भुनाना	Bhuānā
Encourage	प्रोत्साहन देना	Protsāhan denā
Endorse	प्रमाणित करना, दस्तखत करना	Pramanit karanā, Dastkhat karanā
End	अन्त	Ant
Energy	शक्ति	Shakti
Enforce	लागू करना	Lagū karanā
Engage	काम में लगाये रखना	Kām men lagāye rakhanā
Enjoyment	आनन्द	Anānd
Enough	काफी, पर्याप्त	Kāfī, paryapt

266

Enquiry	पूछताछ	*Puchhtāchh*
Enter	प्रवेश	*Pravesh*
Entertain	सत्कार करना	*Satkār karanā*
Envelope	लिफाफा	*Liphāphā*
Epidemic	महामारी	*Mahāmarī*
Erect	सीधा	*Sīdhā*
Error	भूल	*Bhūl*
Equal	समान	*Samān*
Escape	बच निकलना	*Bach nikalnā*
Essential	आवश्यक	*Avshayak*
Estimate	तखमीना, अनुमान	*Takhmīnā, anumān*
Etiquette	शिष्टाचार	*Shistachār*
Evidence	गवाही	*Gavāhī*
Exact	सही, ठीक	*Sahī, thīk*
Examine	परीक्षा लेना	*Parīkshā lenā*
Exceed	अधिक	*Adhik*
Exchange	अदला-बदली	*Adlā-badlī*
Excited	अत्तेजित	*Uttejit*
Exhibition	प्रदर्शनी	*Pradarshanī*
Exist	अस्तित्व होना	*Astiva honā*
Expel	बाहर करना	*Bāhar karanā*
Expenditure	खर्चा	*Kharchā*
Expert	दक्ष	*Daksh*
Explode	फट जाना	*Fat janā*
Exploit	शोषण करना	*Shōsan karanā*
Explore	खोज करना	*Khoj karanā*
Extension	वृद्धि	*Vraddhi*
Extinguish	बुझाना	*Bujhāna*
Extra	फालतू	*Phāltu*
Ear	कान	*Kān*
Extreme	अति	*Ati*

Eyelash	पलक	*Palak*
Eye ball	पुतली	*Putlī*
Eye	आंख, नेत्र	*Ankh, netra*
Eyewitness	चश्मदीद गवाह	*Chashmīd gavah*
Fabric	कपड़ा, ढांचा	*Kaprā, dhānchā*
Fabricated	झूठा, बनावटी	*Jhuthā, banāvtī*
Face	मुख, चेहरा	*Mukh, Chehrā*
Facility	सुविधा	*Suwidhā*
Fact	तथ्य, सच्चाई	*Tathya, Sachchāi*
Fade	मुर्झाना	*Murijhanā*
Fade	असफल	*Asaphal*
Fair	सुन्दर, मेला	*Sundar, melā*
Fair sex	स्त्री जाति	*Siri jāti*
Faith	विश्वास	*Vishvās*
False	झूठा	*Jhuthā*
Familiar	परिचित	*Parichit*
Family	परिवार	*Parivār*
Fanatic	कट्टर	*Kattar*
Fancy	कल्पना	*Kalpanā*
Fan	पंखा	*Pankhā*
Farce	प्रहसन	*Prahasan*
Farming	खेती	*Khetī*
Fault	दोष	*Dosh*
Favour	पक्ष, कृपा	*Paksh, Kripā*
Feast	दावत, भोज	*Davat, Bhōj*
Feature	आकृति	*Akriti*
Fee	फीस, शुल्क	*Feē, Shulk*
Fellow	साथी	*Shāthī*
Female	महिला	*Mahilā*
Few	कुछ	*Kūchh*
Final	अन्तिम	*Antim*

Fine	जुर्माना	*Jurmanā*
Fire	आग	*A āg*
Finger	अंगुली, उंगलि	*Angulī, Ungali*
Firm	अटल, दृढ़	*Atal, Thradh*
First	प्रथम	*Pratham*
Fish	मछली	*Machhalī*
Flag	झंडा, ध्वज	*Jhandā, dhwaj*
Flight	उड़ान	*Urān*
Flood	बाढ़	*Bādh*
Floors	मंजिले	*Manjilēn*
Fluctuate	घटना-बढ़ना	*Ghatnā-bathnā*
Follower	अनुयायी	*Anuyāyī*
Food	खुराक	*Khurāk*
Forego	त्यागना	*Tyāgnā*
Foreign	विदेशी	*Videshī*
Forenoon	दोपहर से पहले	*Dopahar sē pahale*
Forfeit	जब्त करना	*Jabt karanā*
Forger	जाल साज	*Jāl sāj*
Formality	तकल्लुफ	*Takalluf*
Former	पहला	*Pahalā*
Formula	गुर, नियम	*Gur, Niyam*
Fountain	फुहारा	*Phuharā*
Fragile	नाजुक, कोमल	*Nājuk, komal*
Free	आजाद, मुक्त	*Ajād, mukt*
Fundamental	मौलिक, बुनियादी	*Maulik, buniyādī*
Future	भविष्य	*Bhavisya*
Gamble	जुआ	*Juā*
Game	खेल, शिकार	*Khēl, shikār*
Gang	दल, गिरोह	*Dal, girōh*
Gardener	माली	*Mālī*
General	सामन्य	*Sāmanya*

269

Generation	पीढ़ी	Pīdhī
Genuine	वास्तविक	Vāstavik
Germs	रोगाणु	Rogānu
Gift	उपहार	Uphār
Government	सरकार	Sarkār
Group	समुदाय	Samudāy
Growth	वृद्धि	Vraddhi
Guard	पहरेदार	Paharedār
Guarantee	जमानत	Zamānat
Gum	गोंद	Gaund
Gutter	नाली	Nālī
Habitable	रहने योग्य	Rahane yogye
Half yearly	छमाही	Chhamāhī
Hall	बड़ा कमरा	Barā kamarā
Halt	रूकना	Rukanā
Hand	हाथ	Hāth
Handicrafts	हस्तशिल्प	Hastshilp
Handiwork	हस्तकृति	Hastkriti
Hang	फांसी देना	Phānsi denā
Happening	घटना	Ghatnā
Harbour	बन्दरगाह	Bandargāh
Hard currency	दुर्लभ मुद्रा	Durlabh mudrā
Hardship	कठिनाई, मुश्किल	Kathināi-mushkil
Hazard	संकट	Sankat
Harmony	तालमेल	Tālmēl
Head	सर, शीर्षक, प्रमुख	Sar, shīrshak, pramukh
Head strong	हठी	Hathī
Hear	सुनना	Sunanā
Hearsay	सुनी सुनाई बात	Sunī sunaī bāt
Helmet	लोहे का टोप	Lohe kā top

270

Hereditary	पैतृक, पुश्तैनी	*Paitrik pushtainī*
Hindrance	अड़चन	*Arachan*
Hint	संकेत	*Sankēt*
Hire	किराये पर लेना	*Kirāye par lenā*
History	इतिहास	*Itihās*
Hold	पकड़ना	*Pakarnā*
Homage	श्रद्धांजली	*Shraddhānjalī*
Honey	शहद	*Shahad*
Honour	आदर, इज्जत	*Adār, ijjat*
Hood	टोपी	*Tōpī*
Hook	कांटा	*Kāntā*
Hospital	अस्पताल	*Aspatāl*
Hospitality	आतिथ्य	*Atīthya*
Host	मेज़बान	*Majbān*
Hostile	प्रतिकूल	*Pratikūl*
Hostel	विश्राम गृह	*Vishrām grah*
Human	मानव	*Mānav*
Humane	दयामय	*Dayāmay*
Humorous	मज़ाकिया, विनादी	*Mazākiyā, Vinādi*
Idea	विचार, ख्याल	*Vichār, khyāl*
Identity	पहचान	*Pahachān*
Idiot	बेवकूफ	*Bevakūf, Murkh*
Idle	बेकार	*Bekār*
Ignorance	अज्ञानता	*Agyāntā*
Ill	बीमार	*Bīmaā*
Illegal	गैर कानूनी	*Gair kānunī*
Immaterial	तुच्छ	*Tūchchh*
Immigrant	आप्रवासी	*Apravāsi*
Immoral	दुराचारी	*Durāchari*
Implement	लागू करना	*Lāgu karanā*
Instrument	औजार	*Aujār*

Impostor	ठग	*Thag*
Impress	प्रभाव डालना	*Prabhāv dālnā*
Impression	प्रभाव	*Prabhāv*
Imprisionment	जेल, सजा	*Jel, Sazā*
Improvement	सुधार	*Sudhār*
Inadequate	अपर्याप्त	*Aparyāpt*
Inademissible	अस्वीकार्य	*Aswīkārya*
Inauguration	उद्घाटन	*Udghātan*
Incident	घटना	*Ghajnā*
Incite	उत्तेजित	*Uttejit*
Incline	झूकना	*Jhuknā*
Incompetence	अयोग्यता	*Ayogyatāa*
Indecent	अश्लील	*Ashlīl*
Indefinite	अनिश्चित	*Anishchit*
Inferior	घटिया	*Ghatiyā*
Inhuman	अमानवीय	*Amānvīya*
Injury	चोट	*Chot*
Injustice	अन्याय	*Anyāy*
Insane	पागल	*Pāgal*
Insist	जोर देना	*Jor denā*
Inspection	निरीक्षण	*Nirīkshān*
Install	स्थापित करना	*Sthāpti karanā*
Instalment	किस्त	*Kist*
Instance	उदाहरण	*Udātharān*
Instructor	शिक्षक	*Shikshak*
Insurance	बीमा	*Bīmā*
Intensity	उग्रता	*Ugratā*
Intention	विचार	*Vichār*
Interest	ब्याज, हित	*Byāj, hit*
Interference	हस्तक्षेप	*Hastakshep*
International	अन्तर्राष्ट्रीय	*Antar-rashtrīya*

Interpret	व्याख्या करना	*Vyākhyā karanā*
Internal	आन्तरिक	*Antarik*
Interrogate	पूछताछ	*Pūchhtāchh*
Interrupt	रोकना,	*Rokanā,*
	बाधा डालना	*Bāddhā, dālnā*
Interval	मध्यावकाया	*Madhyāvakāyā*
Intervention	हस्तक्षेप	*Hastakshep*
Interview	मुलाकात	*Mūlākāt*
Intimate	गहरा, घनिष्ट	*Gaharā, ghanist*
Intoxicating	मादक	*Mādak*
Introduction	परिचय,	*Parichay*
Invalidate	रद् करना	*Radd karanā*
Involve	फंसाना	*Phansāna*
Eradication	मिटाना, निर्मूलन	*Mitānā, Nirmulan*
Irregular	अनियमित	*Aniyamit*
Irrelevant	असंगत	*Asangat*
Irreligious	अधार्मिक	*Adhārmik*
Issue	विवादनीय,	*Vivādniy,*
	जारी करना	*Jāri karanā*
Item	मद, वस्तु	*Mad, vastu*
jacket	छोटा, कोट	*Chhotā kot*
Joint	जोड़ संयुक्त	*Jor, sanyukt*
Journal	पत्रिका	*Patrikā*
Journalist	पत्रकार	*Patrakār*
Judge	न्यायाधीश	*Nyāyādhīsh*
Judicial	न्यायिक	*Nyāyik*
Junction	स्टेशन जहां कई	*Station jahān kaī*
	गाड़िया आती है	*gārihān atī hain*
Junior	छोटा	*Chhotā*
Keen	उत्सुक	*Utsūk*
Keep	रखना	*Rakhanā*

Keeper	पालक	*Pālak*
Key	चाबी	*Chābī*
Kidnap	अपहरण करना	*Apaharan karanā*
Kidney	गुर्दा	*Gurdā*
Kind	दयालु	*Dayālu*
Kit	यात्रा का समान	*Yātrā kā samān*
Kitchen	रसोईघर	*Rasoīghar*
Knot	गांठ	*Gānth*
Knowledge	ज्ञान	*Gyān*
Kith & kin	निकट सम्बन्धी	*Nikat sambandhī*
Laborious	परिश्रमी	*Parishramī*
Labour	श्रम	*Shram*
Labourer	श्रमिक, मजदूर	*Shramik, mazdūr*
Lack	अभाव, कमी	*Abhāv, kamī*
Lady	महिला	*Mahilā*
Land	भूमि	*Bhūmi*
Land Lord	ज़मींदार	*Jammīndār*
Land Lady	मालकिन	*Mālkin*
Large	बड़ा, विशाल	*Barā, Vishāl*
Late	देर से, स्वर्गीय	*Der se, swargīy*
Later	पिछला, बाद वाला	*Pichhalā, Bād wālā*
Latest	अन्तिम, आखरी	*Antim, ākhirī*
Lavatory	पखाना, शौचालय	*Pakhanā, shauchalāy*
Lavish	उदार	*Udār*
Law	विधि, नियम	*Vidhi, Niyam*
Lawyer	वकील	*Vakīl*
Lead	अगवाई, नेतृत्व	*Agavāī, Netratva*
	मार्ग दिखलाना	*Mārg dikhlanā*
Leader	नेता	*Netā*
Leave	छुट्टी	*Chhuttī*
Legal	कानूनी	*Kānunī*

Legitimate	जायज़, उचित	*Jāyaz, Uchit*
Lenient	उदार, नरम	*Udār, naram*
Level	स्तर	*Star*
Liberty	स्वतन्त्रता	*Swatantratā*
Life	जीवन	*Jīwan*
Likelihood	संभावना	*Sambhāvanā*
Limit	सीमा, हद	*Sīmā, had*
List	सूची	*Suchī*
Local	स्थानीय	*Sthānīya*
Loose	ढीला	*Dhīlā*
Loss	हानि, नकुसान	*Hāni, Nukasān*
Lower	निचला	*Nichlā*
Luxury	विलास	*Vilās*
Location	स्थान	*Sthān*
Loyalty	वफादार	*Vaphādār*
Madam	महोदया	*Mahodayā*
Maintain	बनाये रखना	*Banāye rakhanā*
Major	बालिग, मेजर	*Bālig, Major*
Management	प्रबन्ध	*Praband*
Manner	ढंग	*Dhang*
Manufacture	निर्माण	*Nirmān*
Map	नक्शा	*Nakshā*
Mark	निशान	*Nishān*
Mate	साथी	*Sāthī*
Mattress	चटाई	*Chatāī*
Maximum	अधिकतम	*Adhiktam*
Measure	उपाय, नाप	*Upāy, Nāp*
Meeting	सभा	*Sabhā*
Member	सदस्य	*Sadasya*
Mental	मानसिक	*Mānsik*
Merge	मिलाना	*Milānā*

Merit	योग्यता	*Yogyatā*
Mess	भोजनालय	*Bhojanalāya*
Message	संदेश	*Sandesh*
Mild	हल्का	*Halkā*
Minimum	कम से कम	*Kam se kam*
Minister	मंत्री	*Mantrī*
Ministry	मंत्रालय	*Mantrālay*
Minor	नाबालिग, छोटा	*Nābālig, Chotā*
Misbehaviour	दुर्व्यवार	*Durvayavhār*
Mischief	शरारत	*Sharārat*
Missionary	धर्म, प्रचारक	*Dharm pracharāk*
Mistake	गलती	*Galtī*
Misuse	दुरूपयोग	*Durpayog*
Mixed	मिला-जुला	*Milā-julā*
Modify	संशोधन	*Sanshodhan*
Monetary	आर्थिक	*Arthik*
Money	धन	*Dhan*
Monthly	मासिक	*Māsik*
Mode	रीति, ढंग	*Rīti, dhang*
Mobile	चलता-फिरता	*Chaltā-phirtā*
Modification	संशोधन, सुधार	*Sanshodhan, Sudhār*
Most	अधिक	*Adhik*
Movable	चल	*Chal*
Move	चलना	*Chalnā*
Movement	आन्दोलन	*Andolan*
Movie	सिनेमा	*Cinemā*
Mule	खच्चर	*Khachchar*
Multiple	बहुमुखी	*Bahumukhī*
Murder	हत्या	*Hatyā*
Murderer	हत्यारा	*Hatyārā*
Museum	अजायबघर	*Ajāyabghar*

276

Music	संगीत	*Sangīt*
Myself	स्वचं मैं	*Swaym, main*
Mythology	पौराणिक	*Paurānik*
Nail	कील, नाखून	*Kīl, Nākhun*
Narration	वर्णन	*Varnan*
Narrow	तंग, संकीर्ण	*Tang, Sankīrn*
Nation	राष्ट्र, कौम	*Rāstr, Kaūm*
National	राष्ट्रीय	*Rāstrīya*
Natural	स्वाभाविक	*Swabhāvik*
Nature	स्वभाव, प्रकृति	*Swabhāv, prakriti*
Navigation	नाविकज्ञान	*Nāvikgyān*
Neat	साफ-स्वच्छ	*Sāf, Swachchh*
Necessary	आवश्यक	*Āvashyak*
Necessity	आचश्यकता	*Āvashyakta*
Need	आचश्यकता	*Āvashyakta*
Needy	जरूरतमन्द	*Jaruratmand*
Neglect	उपेक्षा करना	*Upekshā karanā*
Negligence	लापरवाही,	*Lāparvāhi,*
	उपेक्षा	*Upekshā*
Negotiate	बात-चीत करना	*Bāt-chīt karanā*
Nervous	घबराना	*Ghabarānā*
Neutral	तटस्थ	*Tatasth*
News	समाचार	*Samāchār*
Night	रात	*Rāt*
Nonsense	व्यर्थ	*Vyarth*
Notice	सुचना, नोटिस	*Suchanā, Nōtis*
Numerous	अनेक, बहुत से	*Anek, bahut sē*
Nurse	नर्स	*Nars*
Oath	शपथ	*Shapath*
Obedience	आज्ञा पालन	*Āgyā pālan*
Obedient	आज्ञाकारी	*Āgyākarī*

Object	वस्तु, इरादा,	*Vastu, Irādā*
	एतराज करना	*Etarāj karanā*
Objection	एतराज	*Etarāj*
Obligaiton	आभार	*Abhār*
Observe	देखना	*Dekhanā*
Obstacle	रूकावट	*Rukāvat*
Obstruction	बाधा, रूकावट	*Bādhā, rukāvat*
Obtain	प्राप्त करना	*Prāpt karanā*
Occasion	अवसर, मौका	*Avasar, Maūkā*
Occupation	पेशा, धंधा	*Peshā, dhandhā*
Occupy	कब्जा करना	*Kabjā karanā*
Occur	घटित होना	*Ghatit honā*
Offence	अपराध, जुर्म	*Aprādh, jurm*
Officer	अधिकारी	*Adhikāri*
Official	सरकारी	*Sarkāri*
Old	प्रचीन, बुढ़ा	*Prachīn, Budhā*
Omission	भूल-चूक	*Bhul-chuk*
Opinion	मत, राय	*Mat, Rāy*
Oppose	विरोध	*Virōdh*
Oral	ज़बानी	*Zabāni*
Operate	लागू करना	*Lāgu karanā*
	काम करना	*Kām karanaā*
Operation	चीरा	*Chīrā*
Order	आदेश, आज्ञा	*Ādesh, Āgyā*
Ordinary	साधारण	*Sādharān*
Organization	संगठन	*Sangathan*
Otherwise	अन्यथा	*Anyathā*
Outside	बाहर	*Bāhar*
Over	ऊपर, समाप्त	*Upar, samāpt*
Over crowding	बहुत भीड़ होना	*Bahut bhīt honā*
Overlook	उपेक्षा	*Upekshā*

Over run	कुचल देना	*Kuchal denā*
Over turn	उलट देना	*Ulat denā*
Owe	आभारी होना	*Ābhāri honā*
Ownership	मिलकियत	*Milkiyat*
Oxygen	आक्सीजन	*Āksījan*
Package	गठरी, बण्डल	*Gatharī, badal*
Packet	छोटा डिब्बा	*Chhotā, dibbā*
Paint	रंग	*Rang*
Pair	जोड़ा	*Jorā*
Panic	आतंक	*Ātank*
Paper	कागज़	*Kagaz*
Parallel	समानान्तर	*Samānāntar*
Parasite	परजीवी	*Purjīwī*
Pardon	क्षमा	*Kshamā*
Particular	विशेष	*Vishēsh*
Party	दल	*Dal*
Passage	मार्ग, रास्ता	*Mārg, Rāstā*
Path	मार्ग	*Mārg*
Patient	रोगी	*Rogī*
Patron	संरक्षक	*Sanrakshak*
Pattern	नमूना	*Namunā*
Pauper	बहुत गरीब	*Bahut garīb*
Pavement	पटरी	*Patarī*
Pavillion	मंडप, बैठने का स्थान	*Mandap, Baithne kā Sthān*
Pay	वेतन -तनख्वाह	*Vetan, Tankhvah*
Payee	पाने वाला	*Pāne wālā*
Payment	भुगतान	*Bhugtān*
Pedestrian	पैदल चलने वाला	*Paidal chaine wālā*
Penalty	दंड	*Dand*

Pending	विचारधीन	*Vicharādhīn*
Per-annum	प्रतिवर्ष	*Prativarsh*
Per cent	प्रतिशत	*Pratishat*
Perfection	पूर्णता	*Purntā*
Perfect	पूर्ण	*Pūrn*
Perform	पूरा करना	*Purā karanā*
Perhaps	शायद	*Shāyad*
Period	अवधि	*Avadhi*
Permanent	स्थायी	*Sthāyi*
Permission	अनुमति	*Anumati*
Personal	निजी	*Nijī*
Personality	व्यक्तित्व	*Vyaktitya*
Petty	छोटा	*Chhotā*
Pilgrimage	तीर्थ यात्रा	*Tīrth yātrā*
Policy	नीति	*Nīti*
Popular	लोकप्रिय	*Lokpriya*
Population	जनसंख्या	*Jansankhyā*
Portfolio	विभाग	*Vibhāg*
Portions	भाग, हिस्से	*Bhāg, hisse*
Position	स्थान, स्थिति	*Sthān, Sthiti*
Possession	अधिकार, कब्जा	*Adhikār, Kabjā*
Post-Telegraph	डाक–तार	*Dāk-tār*
Postman	डाकिया	*Dakiyā*
Post office	डाकघर	*Dākghar*
Postpone	स्थगित करना	*Sthagit karnā*
Posture	ढंग–भाव	*Dhang-bhāv*
Percaution	एहतियात	*Ethtiyāt*
Precede	पहिले होना	*Pahile honā*
Prefer	अधिक पसन्द करना	*Adhik pasand karanā*
Pre-occupation	व्यस्तता	*Vyastatā*

Prepared	तैयार	*Taiyār*
Presence	उपस्थिति	*Upasthiti*
Prestige	मान गौरव	*Mān gōrav*
Presumption	अनुमान	*Anumān*
Pretence	बहाना	*Bahānā*
Prevalent	प्रचलित	*Prachit*
Prevent	रोकना	*Rokanā*
Previous	पहले का	*Pahale kā*
Primary	प्राथमिक	*Prātmik*
Private	निजी	*Nijī*
Prize	इनाम, पुरस्कार	*Inām, Puraskār*
Problem	समस्या	*Samasyā*
Profession	पेशा	*peshā*
Programme	प्रोग्राम	*Progrām*
Progress	प्रगति	*Pragti*
Prominent	प्रमुख	*Pramūkh*
Proof	प्रमाण	*Pramān*
Proposal	प्रस्ताव	*Prastāv*
Protect	रक्षा करना	*Rakshā karanā*
Protest	विरोध करना	*Virodh karanā*
Provide	व्यवस्था करना	*Vyavasthā karanā*
Punctual	समय का पाबन्द	*Samay kā paband*
Punishment	सजा	*Sazā*
Purchase	खरीदना	*Kharīdnā*
Pure	शुद्ध	*Shuddh*
Pursue	पीछा करना	*Pīchhā karnā*
Quack	ढोंगी डाक्टर	*Shōngī doctor*
Qualification	योग्यता	*Yogyatā*
Qualified	योग्य	*Yogya*
Quality	गुण	*Guna*
Quantity	मात्रा, मिकदार	*Mātrā, Mikdār*

Quarterly	तिमाही	*Timāhi*
Queen	रानी	*Rānī*
Query	प्रश्न	*Prashn*
Question	प्रश्न	*Prashn*
Quick	जल्दी, तेज	*Jaldi, tej*
Quit	छोड़ देना	*Chhor denā*
Rain	वर्षा	*Varsā*
Rank	पदवी	*Padvī*
Rape	बलात्कार	*Balātkār*
Rapid	शीध्र	*Shīghra*
Rate	भाव	*Bhāv*
Rate of Exchange	विनिमय दर	*Kinimay dar*
Raw	कच्चा	*Kachchā*
Reach	पहुंचना	*Pahunchnā*
Read	पढ़ना	*Padhanā*
Ready	तैयार	*Taiyār*
Real	असली, वास्तविक	*Aslī, Vāstvik*
Realize	अनुभव करना,	*Anubhav karanā,*
	वसूल करना	*Vasul karanā*
Reasonable	उचित	*Uchit*
Receive	प्राप्त करना	*Prāpt karanā*
Recent	तत्कालिक	*Tatkālik*
Reception	स्वागत	*Swāgat*
Recital	पाठ	*Pāth*
Recognise	पहिचानना	*Pahichānanā*
Recollect	याद करना	*Yād karanā*
Recommend	सिफरिश करना	*Sifarish karanā*
Reconsider	फिर से विचार	*Phir sē vichār*
	करना	*karanā*
Record	अभिलेख	*Abhilekh*
Recover	वसूल करना	*Vasul karanā*

Recreation	मनोरंजन	*Manoranjan*
Recruit	भर्ती करना	*Bharti karanā*
Rectify	सुधारना	*Sudhārnā*
Reduce	कम करना	*Kam karanā*
Refer	हवाला देना	*Hawāla denā*
Refund	रूपये की वापसी	*Rupaye ki vāpsī*
Refuse	इन्कार करना	*Inkār karanā*
Refuse	कूड़ा	*Kurā*
Regard	आदर	*Adar*
Region	प्रदेश	*Pradesh*
Regret	अफसोस करना	*Afsos karanā*
Regular	नियमित	*Niyamat*
Reject	नामंजूर करना	*Namanjur karana*
Relax	शरीर को आराम देना	*Sharir ko ārām denā*
Release	रिहाई देना	*Rehāri Denā*
Relevant	उचित, संगत	*Uchit, Sangat purn*
Relief	सहायता, आराम	*Sahaytā, Arām*
Religion	धार्मिक	*Dhārmik*
Remainder	बाकी, अवशेष	*Bākī, avshesh*
Remedy	उपाय	*Upāy*
Remind	याद दिलाना	*Yād dilana*
Remove	हटाना	*Hatānā*
Renew	चालू करना, नया करना	*Chālu karanā, Nayā karanā*
Rent	किराया	*Kirāyā*
Repairs	मरम्मत	*Marammat*
Repay	चुकाना	*Chukānā*
Repeat	दोहराना	*Doharanā*
Replace	बदलना	*Badalnā*

Reputation	ख्याति	*Khyāti*
Request	प्रार्थना	*Prārthnā*
Rescue	बचाना	*Bachānā*
Residence	निवास	*Nivās*
Respectfully	आदरपूर्वक	*Adār purvak*
Respectively	यथाक्रम	*Yathā kram*
Responsible	उत्तरदायी	*Uttardayī*
Restore	लौटाना	*Lautāna*
Restrict	सीमित करना	*Sīmit karanā*
Restriciton	पाबन्दी	*Pābandī*
Result	फल	*Phal*
Resume	फिर शुरू करना	*Phir shuru karanā*
Retail	फुटकर व्यापार	*Phutkar vyāpār*
Return	वापसी, विवरण पत्र	*Vāpasi, Vivaran Patra*
Reverse	उल्टा	*Ultā*
Revise	दोहराना	*Doharānā*
Reward	इनाम	*Inām*
Right	ठीक, दाहिना	*Thīk, Dāhinā*
Riot	दंगा	*Dangā*
Risk	जोखिम	*Jōkhim*
Road	सड़क	*Sarak*
Robbery	लूटमार	*Lutmār*
Room	कमरा	*Kamarā*
Rotten	गला हुआ	*Galā huā*
Rough	खुरदरा	*Khurdurā*
Round	गोल, चारों तरफ	*Gol, Chāron taraf*
Route	मार्ग, रास्ता	*Mārg, Rāstā*
Routine	सामान्य काम	*Sāmānya kām*
Rub	रगड़ना	*Ragaranā*
Rule	नियम, शासन	*Niyam, Shāsan*

Rupture	फट जाना	*Phai janā*
Rural	ग्रामीण	*Grāmin*
Rustic	गंवार	*Ganvār*
Sabotage	तोड़ -फोड़	*Torphor*
Sacred	पवित्र	*Pavitra*
Safe	सुरक्षित, तिजोरी	*Surakshit, Tijōrī*
Sale	बिक्री	*Bikrī*
Same	वही	*Vahī*
Sample	नमूना	*Namunā*
Sanction	मजुर, स्वीकृति	*Manjur, Swīkriti*
Sanitary	स्वास्थ्य, सफाई	*Swāsthya, Safāi*
Saving	बचत	*Bachat*
Satisfaction	संतोष	*Santosh*
Satisfactory	संतोषजनक	*Santoshjanak*
Scale	पैमाना, तराजू	*Paimānā, Tarāju*
Scandal	बदनामी का काम	*Badnāmi kā kām*
Scanty	थोड़ा कम	*Thorā kam*
Scarcity	कमी	*Kamī*
Scatter	बखेरना	*Bakheranā*
Scene	दृश्य, स्थान	*Drashy, Sthān*
Schedule	अनुसूची	*Anusuchi*
Scheme	योजना	*Yojanā*
Search	तलाश, खोज	*Talās, Khoj*
Season	मौसम	*Mausam*
Seclusion	एकान्त	*Ekānt*
Second	दुसरा	*Dusarā*
Secondary	माध्यमिक	*Mādhyamik*
Secret	रहस्य, राज़	*Rahasya, Rāj*
Secretary	सचिव	*Sachiv*
Section	विभाग	*Vibhāg*
Secular	धर्म निरपेक्ष	*Dharm Nirpeksh*

Secure	सुरक्षित,	*Surakshit*
	प्राप्त करना	*Prāpt karna*
See	देखना	*Dekhnā*
Seize	कब्जा करना	*Kabjā karanā*
Select	चूनना,	*chunanā, Pasand*
	पसन्द करना	*karanā*
Sell	बेचना	*Bechanā*
Send	भेजना	*Bhejanā*
Sentence	जुमला, वाक्य,	*Jumlā, Vākya,*
	सज़ा	*Sazā*
Separate	अलग, पृथक	*Alag, Prathak*
Septic	ज़हर फैलना	*Zahar phailnā,*
	पीप भरना	*Pip Barnā*
Sequence	सिलसिला	*Silsilā*
Service	सेवा, नौकरी	*Sevā, Naukarī*
Settle	बसना	*Basnā*
Several	अनेक	*Anek*
Severe	कड़ा, सख्त	*Korā, sakht*
Sex	लिंग भेद	*Ling bhed*
Sexual	काम सम्बन्धी	*Kām Sambandhi*
Shall	गा,गे,गी	*Gā, ge, gī*
Shame	शर्म, धिक्कार	*Sharm, dhikkār*
Shape	आकार	*Akār*
Share	हिस्सा, भाग	*Hissā, Bhāg*
Shelf	अलमारी	*Almārī*
Shift	पारी, हट जाना	*Pārī, hat jānā*
Ship	जहाज	*Jahāj*
Shock	सदमा, धक्का	*Sadmā, Dhakkā*
Shoe	जूता	*Jutā*
Shoot	उगना, गोली	*Ugnā, goli marnī*
Shortage	कमी	*Kamī*

Shoulder	कन्धा	*Kandhā*
Sick	रोगी, बीमार	*Rogī, Bimār*
Sign	हस्ताक्षर	*Hastākshar*
	करना	*Karnā*
Signature	हस्ताक्षर	*Hastākshar*
Significant	महत्वपूर्ण	*Mahatvapurn*
Similar	समान, एकसा	*Samān, Eksā*
Simple	सीधा-सादा	*Sīdha-sadā*
Since	क्योंकि, चूँकि	*Kyonki, chunki*
Sincerely	सच्चाई से	*Sachchāi se*
Single	एक, अकेला	*Ek, akelā*
Sir	श्रीमान्	*Shrimān*
Sister	नर्स, बहिन	*Nars, bahin*
Sit	बैठना	*Baithnā*
Site	स्थान	*Sthān*
Six	छै:	*Chhai*
Situated	स्थित	*Sthit*
Situation	स्थिति	*Sthiti*
Skill	कला, हुनर	*Kalā, hunar*
Skin	चमड़ी	*Chamrī*
Sky	आकाश, आसमान	*Akāsh, asmān*
Slaughter	वध	*Vadh*
Slip	पर्ची, खिसकना	*Parchī, Kiskanā*
Slogan	नारा	*Nārā*
Slope	ढ़ाल	*Dhāl*
Small	छोटा या छोटी	*Chhotā yā chhotī*
Smuggle	चोरी से लाना	*Chorī se lanā*
Social	सामाजिक	*Sāmājik*
Solution	समाधान, हल	*Sāmadhān, hal*
Sort	छांटना किस्म	*Chhātnā, kism*
Source	निकास, जरिया	*Nikās, Jariyā*

287

South	दक्षिण	*Dakshin*
Spare	फालतू	*Phaltu*
Special	विशेष	*Vishesh*
Specific	विशिष्ट	*Vishist*
Speed	रफतार, चाल	*Raftar, chal*
Spittoon	थूकदान	*Thukdan*
Spot	स्थान, निशान	*Sthan, Nishan*
Squat	पालथी मार कर बैठना	*Palthi mar kar baithana*
Squeeze	निचोड़ना	*Nichorna*
Stability	स्थिरता	*Sthirta*
Stack	ढेर, अम्बार	*Dher ambar*
Staff	अमला, कर्मचारी	*Amla, karmchari*
Stage	रंग-मंच	*Rangmanch*
Stagger	लड़खाना	*Larkharana*
Stain	धब्बा, दाग	*Dhabba, dag*
Stair Case	जीना, सीढ़ी	*Jina, sidi*
Stamp	डाक टिकट	*Dak Ticket*
Stand	स्टाप, अड्डा	*Stap, adda*
Stand	खड़ा होना	*Khara hona*
Standard	स्तर, दर्जा	*Star, darji*
State	राज्य	*Rajya*
Statement	बयान, वक्तव्य	*Bajan, Vaktavya*
Statue	मूर्ति	*Murti*
Statute	कानून	*Kanun*
Stay	ठहरना, स्थागन	*Thaharna Sthagan*
Steady	दृढ़	*Dradh*
Steam	भाप	*Bhap*
Step	कदम	*Kadam*
Sterile	बांझ	*Banjh*
Steward	खानसामा	*Khansama*

Stipend	वजीफा	*Vajifā*
Stirrup	रकाब	*Rakāb*
Storm	तूफान	*Tuphān*
Straight	सीधा	*Sidhā*
Strain	तनाव, भारीपन	*Tanāv, Bhārīpan*
Strange	अनोखा, अजब	*Anokhā, Ajab*
Strap	तसमा	*Tasmā*
Strength	तख्त	*Takat*
Stress	जोर देना	*Jor denā*
Struggle	सधर्ष	*Sangharsh*
Style	दंग	*Dhang*
Subject	विषय	*Vishay*
Submit	निविदा करना	*Nivedān karanā*
Subordinate	अधीन	*Adhīn*
Subscription	चन्दा	*Chandā*
Subsidy	सरकारी मदद	*Sarkārī madad*
Substitute	बदले में	*Badle men*
Succession	उत्तराधिकार	*Uttarādhikār*
Sudden	अचानक	*Achānak*
Sue	दवा करना	*Davā karanā*
Sufficient	काफी	*Kāfī*
Sun-Stroke	लू लगना	*Lu laganā*
Superficial	दिखावटी	*Dikhāvatī*
Superior	बढ़िया, बड़ा	*Badhiyā, Barā*
Superstitious	अंधविश्वास	*Andvishvās*
Supply	समन देना, पूर्ति	*Saman denā, Purti*
Support	अधर, सहायता	*Adhar, Sahāyatā*
Suppress	दमन	*Daman*
Surface	सतह, तल	*Satah, Tal*
Surprise	आश्चर्य	*Ashcharya*
Surrender	सम्पर्ण	*Samarpan*

Suspect	शंका करना	*Shankā karanā*
Suspicious	संशयप्रद	*Sanshayaprad*
Symptom	लक्षण	*Lakshān*
Syringe	पिचकारी	*Pichkārī*
System	तारीका, दंग	*Tārīkā, Dhang*
Systematic	ढ़ग से	*Dhang se*
Table	मेज	*Mej*
Tablet	टिकिया	*Tikiyā*
Tackle	सभालना	*Sambhālnā*
Tact	होशियारी	*Hoshiyārī*
Tactful	होशियार	*Hōshiyār*
Take	लेना	*Lenā*
Talent	अक्ल, बुद्धि	*Akal, buddhi*
Tamper	खराब करना	*Kharāb karanā*
Tap	नलका	*Nalkā*
Target	निशान	*Nishān*
Tax	कर	*Kar*
Tariff	चुंगी कर	*Chungī kar*
Task	कार्यभार	*Kārya bhār*
Tea	चाय	*Chāy*
Telegram	तार	*Tār*
Telegraph Office	तारघर	*Tār ghar*
Temperature	तापमान	*Tāpmān*
Temporary	अस्थायी	*Asthāyi*
Test	परीक्षा	*Parīkshā*
Texture	बनावट	*Banāvat*
Thereby	उससे	*Usase*
Therefore	इसलिये	*Isaliye*
Thereof	उसका	*Uskā*
Thereon	उस पर	*Us par*
Thorough (ly)	पूरा, पूरी तरह	*Purā, purī tarah*

Threat	धमकी	*Dhamkī*
Through	द्वारा	*Dvārā*
Thumb	अंगूठा	*Anguthā*
Tied	बंधा हुआ	*Bandhā huā*
Time	समय	*Samay*
Together	साथ-साथ	*Sāth-Sāth*
Tongue	जुबान, जीभ	*Jubān, Jībh*
Top	चोटी, लट्टू	*Chotī, lattu*
Torrent	तेज धारा	*Tej dhārā*
Total	जोड़, योग	*Jor yōg*
Tour	दौरा, यात्रा	*Daurā, yātrā*
Town	नगर, शहर	*Nagar, Shahr*
Tradition	परम्परा	*Parmparā*
Traffic	यातायात	*Yātāyāt*
Transfer	तबादला	*Tabādlā*
Translation	अनुवाद	*Anuvād*
Transport	परिवहन	*Parivahan*
Tremor	थरथरी	*Thartharī*
Tribal	आदिम जाति	*Adām jāti*
Trousers	पाजामा	*Pājāmā*
True	सच्चा	*Sachchā*
Truly	सचमुच, सचाई	*Sachmuch, sachāī*
Trust	विश्वास, भरोसा	*Vishvās, bharosā*
Tunnel	सुरंग	*Surang*
Twice	दुबारा	*Subārā*
Typical	स्वाभाविक	*Swābhāvik*
Ultimate	अन्तिम	*Antim*
Unable	असमर्थ	*Asmarth*
Unanimous	एकमत	*Ekmat*
Unauthorised	बिना अधिकार	*Binā adhikār*
Unavoidable	अनिवार्य	*Anivārya*

Unaware	बेखबर	*Bekhabar*
Uncertain	अनिश्चित	*Anischit*
Unclaimed	लावारिस	*Lāvaris*
Unconditional	बिना शर्त	*Binā shart*
Under	नीचे	*Nīche*
Undergo	सहना	*Sahanā*
Understanding	समझ	*Samajh*
Undesirable	अनुचित	*Anuchit*
Undeveloped	अविकसित	*Aviksit*
Undivided	अविभक्त	*Avibhakt*
Undoubtedly	नि:सन्देह	*Nisandeh*
Undue	अनुचित	*Anuchit*
Unequal	बेजोड़	*Bejor*
Unfair	अनुचित	*Anuchit*
Unfit	अयोग्य	*Ayogya*
Unique	अपूर्व,अजब	*Apurv, Ajab*
Unit	इकाई, एक भाग	*Ikat, ek bhāg*
Universal	विश्वव्यापी	*Vishvavyāpī*
Unjust	अन्यायपूर्ण	*Anyāyapurn*
Unlawful	गैर कानूनी	*Gair kānunī*
Unnatural	अप्राकृतिक	*Aprākritik*
Unlikely	गैर मुमकिन	*Gair mumkin*
Unreasonable	अनुचित	*Anuchit*
Unreliable	अविश्वसनीय	*Avishvasnīya*
Unskilled	अकुशल	*Akushal*
Until	जब तक	*Jabtak*
Uplift	तरक्की	*Tarakkā*
Urban	शहरी	*Shaharā*
Urgency	बहुत जरूरी	*Bahut zarurā*
Urinal	पेशाब घर	*Peshābghar*
Urine	पेशाब, मूत्र	*Peshāb, Mutra*

292

Use	उपयोग	*Upayōg*
Usual	साधारण, मामूली	*Sadhārān, māmuli*
Utilise	उपयोग करना	*Upayog karanā*
Vacant	खाली, रिक्त	*Khāli, rikt*
Vacation	छुट्टियां	*Chhuttiyān*
Vaccination	टीका	*Tīkā*
Vague	अस्पष्ट	*Aspasht*
Valid	सही, जायज	*Sahā, jāyaz*
Valuable	कीमती चीज़	*Kāmtā chāj*
Variation	तब्दीलियां	*Tabdāliyān*
Variety	विभेद	*Vibhed*
Vary	बदलना	*Badalnā*
Vast	बड़ा	*Barā*
Venture	साहसी काम	*Sāhasī kām*
Venue	स्थान	*Sthān*
Veracity	सच्चाई	*Sachchāi*
Verbal	शब्दों में	*Shabdon men*
Verbally	ज़बान से	*Jabān se*
Verification	जांच	*Jānch*
Verify	तसदीक करना	*Tasdik Karana*
	पड़ताल करना	*Portāl karanā*
Via	द्वारा	*Dwārā*
Vibration	कम्पन	*Kampan*
Vice	बुराई, बरी आदत	*Burāi, burī adat*
Viceversa	उल्टा	*Ultā*
Vicinity	पड़ौस	*Paraus*
Vigilance	देखभाल	*Dekhbhāl*
Vigorous	मेहनत से भरा,	*Mahnat se bharā*
	जोरदार	*Jordār*
Village	ग्राम, गांव	*Grām gānv*
Vindicate	सही साबित	*Sahī sābit karana*
	करना	*Bachav karana*

Violate	भंग करना	*Bhang karanā*
	कानून तोड़ना	*Kānoon Todnā*
Violence	हिंसा	*Hinsā*
Virus	जहरवाद, सवाद	*Jaharvād, mavād*
Visit	मिलने जाना या आना	*Milne janā yā anā*
Visitor	मिलनेवाला	*Milnewalā*
Vital	बहुत महत्त्वपूर्ण	*Bahut mahatvapurn*
Volume	परिमान, पुस्तक	*Parimān, Pustak*
Vulgar	अश्लील असभ्य	*Ashlīl asabhya*
Waiting list	पृष्ट सूची	*Pritisha suchī*
Week	सप्ताह	*Saptāh*
Weekly	सप्ताहिक	*Saptāhik*
Weight	वजन, भार	*Vazan, bhār*
Welfare	भलाई, हित	*Bhalāī, hit*
Western	पश्चिमी	*Pashchimī*
West	पश्चिम	*Pashchim*
Whereabouts	पता, ठिकाना	*Patā, Thikānā*
White	सफेद	*Saphed*
Whole	पूरा, सारा	*Purā, Sārā*
Windfall	अचानक पैसा आना	*Achānak paisā anā*
Wing	बाजू, पक्ष	*Bāju, paksh*
Winter	शीतल, सर्दी	*Shītkal, Sardī*
Wipe	पहुँचना, मिटाना	*Ponchhanā, mitānā*
Wireless	बेतार का तार	*Betār kā tār*
Withdraw	वापस लेना	*Vāpas lena*
Withoutfail	हर हाल में, जरूर	*Har hāl men, jarur*
Witness	गवाह, साक्षी	*Govāh Sākshī*
Warden	रक्षक, मुहाफिज	*Rakshak, Muhāphiz*
Warder	पहरेदार	*Paharedār*

Wardrobe	कपड़ों की अलमारी	Kaparon kī almarī
Warehouse	गोदाम	Godām
Warning	चेतावनी	Chetāvanī
Warp	ताना बाना	Tānā bānā
Warranty	प्रतिज्ञा	Pratigyā
Wash	धोना	Dhōnā
Waste	बरबाद करना, नष्ट करना	Barbād karnā, Nast karanā
Wastage	बरबादी	Barbādi
Wasteland	बंजर जमीन	Banjar Zamīm
Watch	घड़ी, चौकसी	Gharī, Chaukasī
Watchman	चौकीदार	Chaukīdār
Water	पानी, जल	Pānī, Jal
Water basin	पानी की बात	Pānī kī hāh
Wash basin	धोने की चिमची	Dhone kī (chilmachi)
Waterproof	बरसाती	Barsātī
Water Ways	पानी के रास्ते	Pānī ke rāste
Wave	लहर	Lahar
Weak	कमजोर	Kamzōr
Weapon	हथियार	Hathiyār
Weather	मौसम	Mausam
Wedding	विवाह, शादी	Vivāh, Sādī

PART VII

CHAPTER 44 : Reading Exercise

Chapter 44
Reading Exercise I

मोहन — नमस्ते। आप कैसी है।

कमला — मैं ठीक हूँ, धन्यवाद, आप कैसे है?

मोहन — मैं भी ठीक हूँ। आप के पति कहां है?

कमला — मेरे पति आगरा में हैं।

मोहन — आपका घर कहां है?

कमला — मेरा घर हौजखास में है।

मोहन — आपके कितने बच्चे हैं?

कमला — मेरे चार बच्चे हैं–दो बेटे और दो बेटियां।

मोहन — बच्चों के नाम क्या है?

कमला — लड़को के नाम लव और कुश हैं।

मोहन — और लड़कियों के नाम?

कमला — लड़कियों के नाम गीता और रीता हैं।

मोहन — बहुत सुन्दर नाम हैं आपका घर बड़ा है?

कमला — घर छोटा है, लेकिन बाग बड़ा है।

मोहन — कितने कमरे हैं?

कमला — चार कमरे हैं, एक बैठने-खाने का कमरा, और
तीन सोने के कमरे।

मोहन — आप चाय लेंगी या कुछ ठंडा?

कमला — सिर्फ ठंडा पानी चाहिए।

मोहन — आप फल खाइए। केले बहुत मीठे है।

कमला — आपकी पत्नी और बच्चे कहाँ है?

मोहन — बच्चे स्कूल में है। पत्नी रसोइ। में हैं।

Mohan —	*namaste. āp kaisā hain?*
Kamala —	*main thīk hun, dhanyavād, aur āp kaise hain?*
Mohan —	*main bhī thīk hūm. āpke pati kahām hain?*
Kamala —	*mere patī Āgarā men hain.*
Mohan —	*āpkā ghar kahām hain?*
Kamala —	*merā ghar Hauz Khās men hain.*
Mohan —	*āpke kitna bachche hain?*
Kamala —	*mere chār bachche hain — do bete aur do betiyām.*
Mohan —	*bachchon ke naām kyā hain?*
Kamala —	*larkon ke nām Lav aur Kush hain.*
Mohan —	*aur larkiyon ke nām?*
Kamala —	*larkiyon ke nām Gitā aur Rita hain.*
Mohan —	*bahut sundar nām hin. āpkā ghar barā hai?*
Kamala —	*ghar chhotā hai; lekin bāg barā hai.*
Mohan —	*kitne kamare hain?*
Kamala —	*chār kamaren hain. ek aithane-khane kā kamara, aur tīn sone ke kamare.*
Mohan —	*āp chāy lengī yā kuchh tanda?*
Kamala —	*sirf thandā pānī chāhiya.*
Mohan —	*ap phal khaiye. kele bahut mīthe hain*
Kamala —	*āpkī patnī aur bachche kahan hain?*
Mohan —	*bachche skul men hain. patnī rasoī men hai.*

297

English Translation

Mohan — Namaste. How are you?

Kamala — I am all right, thank you, and how are you?

Mohan — I am all right too. Where is your husband?

Kamala — My husband is in Agra.

Mohan — Where is your house?

Kamala — My house is in Hauz Khas.

Mohan — How many children have you?

Kamala — I have four children—two sns and two daughters.

Mohan — What are the children's names?

Kamala — Boy's names are Lav and Kush.

Mohan — And the girls names?

Kamala — Girls names are Gita and Rita.

Mohan — Names are very pretty. Is your house big?

Kamala — The houose is small, but the garden is big.

Mohan — How many roms are there?

Kamala — There are four rooms. One sitting dining room and theree bed-rooms.

Mohan — Will yu have tea or something cold?

Kamala — I want onlyy cold water.

Mohan — Please eat the fruit. The bananas are very sweet.

Kamala — Where are your wife and children?
Mohan — Children are in the school, wife is in the kichen.

New Words

kaisī	how	कैसी
dhanyavad	thank you	धन्यवाद
āpke	your	आपके
pati	husband	पति
men	in	में
kitane	hoow many	कितने
chār	four	चार
do	two	दो
kyā	what	क्या
dhanyavād	thank you	धन्यवाद
baithane-khāne	sitting-dining	बैठने खाने का
kā kamarā	room	कमरा
sone kā kamarā	bedroom	सोने का कमरा
chāy	tea	चाय
kuchh	some, something	कुछ
thandā	cold	ठंडा
sirf	only	सिर्फ
chāhiye	need, want	चाहिए
khāiye	please eat	खाइये
mīthe	sweet	मीठे
patnī	wife	पत्नी
skul	school	स्कूल
rasoī	kitchen	रसोई

299

अनिल	–	नमस्ते।
डिक	–	नमस्ते।
अनिल	–	आपका शुभ नाम?
डिक	–	मेरा नाम ब्राउन है।
अनिल	–	आप भारत में कब से है?
डिक	–	चार महीने से।
अनिल	–	आप कहां रहते हैं।
डिक	–	अभी तो मैं होटल में रहता हूँ।
अनिल	–	किस होटल में?
डिक	–	जनपथ होटल में।
अनिल	–	अच्छा होटल है?
डिक	–	काफ़ी अच्छा है।
अनिल	–	आप विवाहित है?
डिक	–	जी हाँ। मेरे दो बच्चे भी हैं।
अनिल	–	वे कहां है?
डिक	–	अभी तो वे अमरीका में है।
अनिल	–	वे भारत नहीं आएंगे?
डिक	–	जरूर आएंगे, जब मुझको घर मिलेगा।
अनिल	–	आपको घर कहाँ चाहिए?
डिक	–	सुन्दर नगर, जोरबाग, कहीं भी।
अनिल	–	कैसा घर चाहिए?
डिक	–	कम-से-कम पाँच कमरे होने चाहिए। नौकरों के लिए भी कमरे होने चाहिए।
अनिल	–	शायद मैं आपकी मदद कर सकूं।
डिक	–	बड़ी मेहरबानी होगी। लेकिन मैं आपको तकलीफ़ नहीं देना चाहता।
अनिल	–	तकलीफ़ की कोई बात नहीं।
डिक	–	अच्छी बात है। आपको कोई अच्छा घर मालूम है?
अनिल	–	मैं आपको अपने साथ ले चलूंगा। दो-चार घर दिखाऊंगा।

Anil	—	*namaste.*
Dick	—	*namaste.*
Anil	—	*āpkā shubh nam?*
Dick	—	*merā nām Dick Brown hai.*
Anil	—	*āp Bhārat men kab se hain?*
Dick	—	*char mahine se.*
Anil	—	*āp kahān rahte hain?*
Dick	—	*abhā to main hotal men rahtā hūn.*
Anil	—	*kis hotal men?*
Dick	—	*janpath hotal men.*
Anil	—	*achchā hotal hai?*
Dick	—	*kāfī achchha hai.*
Anil	—	*āp vivāhit hain?*
Dick	—	*jā hān. mere do bachche bhī hain.*
Anil	—	*ve kahān hain?*
Dick	—	*abhī to ve Amarikā men hain.*
Anil	—	*ve Bhārat nahīm āyenge?*
Dick	—	*zarūr āyenge jab mujhko ghar milegā.*
Anil	—	*āpko ghar kahān chahiye?*
Dick	—	*Sundar Nagar, Jorbāg, kahīm bhī.*
Anil	—	*Kaisā ghar chāhiye?*
Dick	—	*kam-se-kam pānch kamare hone chāhiye. naukaron ke liye bhī kamare hone chāhiye.*
Anil	—	*shāyad main āpkī madad kar sakūn.*
Dick	—	*bari meharbānī hogī. lekin main apko taklīf nahīm denā chāhatā.*
Anil	—	*taklīf kī koī bāt nahn.*

Dick — *achchhi b* $\bar{a}$ *t ha* $\overline{i}$, $\bar{a}$ *pko ko* $\overline{i}$ *achchh* $\bar{a}$ *ghar mal* $\overline{u}$ *m hai?*

Anil — *main* $\bar{a}$ *pko apne s* $\bar{a}$ *th le chal* $\overline{u}$ *ng* $\bar{a}$ *do-char ghar dikh* $\overline{a}$ *ung* $\bar{a}$.

English Translation

Anil — Namaste.

Dick — Namaste.

Anil — What is your name, please?

Dick — My name is Dick Brown.

Anil — How long have you been in India?

Dick — For four months.

Anil — Where do you live?

Dick — At the mooment I am staying in a hotel.

Anil — In which hotel?

Dick — In Janpath Hotel.

Anil — Is it a good hotel?

Dick — Is is quite good.

Anil — Are you married?

Dick — Yes. I a have two children.

Anil — Where are they?

Dick — At the moment they are in America.

Anil — Won't they come to India.

Dick — They certainly will, when I get a house.

Anil — Where do you want the house?

Dick — Sundar Nagar, Jogbag, anywhere.

Anil — What sort of a hose do you want?

Dick	—	There should be at least five roms. There shoiuld be rooms for servants to.
Anil	—	May be I can help you.
Dick	—	That will be very kind. But I don't want to trouble you.
Anil	—	There is no trouble at all.
Dick	—	akay then. Do you know of any good house?
Anil	—	I shall take you with me. (I shall) show you a few houses.

New Words

kab se	since when	कब से
vivāhit	married	विवाहित
abhī to	at the moment	अभी तो
kaisā	what sort of	कैसा
kams-se-kam	minimum, at least	कम से कम
shāyad	perhaps	शायद
taklīf	trouble	तकलीफ
malūm	known	मालूम
do-chār	idiomatic way of saying in few	दो चार

303

गरमी के बाद बरसात आती है।
बरसात जुलाई से सितम्बर तक रहती है।
बरसात का मौसम स्वास्थ्य के लिए अच्छा नहीं है।
बीमारियां फैलती हैं।
मक्खी-मच्छर बहुत परेशान करते हैं।
कीड़े-मकोड़े भी बहुत ज्यादा हो जाते हैं।
सब्जी-तरकारी भी अच्छी नहीं मिलती।
सड़कों पर पानी भर जाता है।
लेकिन बरसात बहुत जरूरी भी तो है।
बारिश की पहली बौछार कितनल अच्छी लगती है।
लोग चैन की सांस लेते है।
बच्चे पेड़ों अमरूद और जामून तोड़कर खाते हैं।
बरसात में खाने-पीने में बहुत सावधानरहना चाहिए।
बाजार की चीजें नहीं खानी चाहिए।
उबला पानी पीना चाहिए।

garmī ke bād barsāt ātī hai.
barsāt July se Sitambar tak rahtī hai.
Barsāt kā mausam svāsthya ke liye achchhā nahīn
hai.bīmāriyān phailatī hain.
makkhī-machchhar bahut pareshān karte hain.
kjire-makore bhī bahut zyādā hho jāte hain.
sabzi-tarkārī bhī achchhī nahīn milatī.
sarkon par pani bhar jātā hai.
lekin barasāt bahut zarūrī bhī thai.
bārish kī pahlī bauchhar kitnī achchhī lagaī hai.
log chain kī sāns lete hain.

bachche peron se amrūd aur jāmun tor kar khāte hain.
barsāt men khāne-pīne men bahut sāvadhān rahnā
chahiye.
bāzār kī chizen nahīn khānī chāhiye.
ubalā pānī pīnā chāhiye.

English Translation

The rainy season comes after summer.
The rainy season lasts from July to September.
The rainy season is not good for health.
Diseases spread.
Flies and mosquitoes annoy a lot.
There are too many insects too.
Good vegetables are not available.
Road are full of water.
But the rain is also very essential.
How pleasant are the first showers of rains.
People heave a sigh of relief.
Children pluck guavas and rose apples from trees
and eat.
One should be very careful about what one eats
and drinks in the rainy season.
ne should not eat bazaar things.
Boiled water should be taken.

New Words

ke bād	after	के बाद
se	from	से
tak	up to	तक
svāsthya	health	स्वास्थ्य
phailāti hai	spread	फैलाती है
makkhī	flies	मक्खी
machchhar	mosquitoes	मच्छर

(they are often used as compound word *makkhi-machchhar* to mean both)

kīre	insects	कीड़े
makore	spiders	मकोड़े

(Note the compound word *kire-makore)*

sabzī	green vegetables	सब्जी
tarkārī	general term for	तरकारी

(Note the compound words)

bhar jātā hai	gets filled	भर जाता है
zarūrī	essential	जरूरी
pahlī	first	पहली
bauchhār	showers	बौछार
kitanī	how much	कितनी
chain	relief	चैन
sāns	breath	सांस
amarūd	guavas	अमरूद
jāmun	rose apple	जामुन
tor kar	pluck	तोड़कर
khānāpīnā	eating-drinking	खाना-पीना
ubalā (int.v)	boiled	उबला

306

Reading Exercise IV

पंकज	–	अपम राम को जानते है?
कमल	–	जी नहीं, मैं नहीं जानता।
पंकज	–	वह आपके पड़ोस में रहता है।
कमल	–	मुझको अफसोस है कि मैं उससे कभी नहीं मिला।
पंकज	–	आप उससे जरूर मिलिए। वह मेरा दोस्त है।
कमल	–	जरूर मिलूँगा।
पंकज	–	राम बहुत दिलचस्प आदमी है।
कमल	–	बहुत अच्छी बात है।
पंकज	–	मैं राम को पिछले पंद्रह सालों से जानता हूँ।
कमल	–	क्या आ साथ-साथ पढ़ते थे?
पंकज	–	जी हां, हम एक ही कालिज मे पढ़ते थे।
कमल	–	कृपा कर के उनका पता दीजिए। उनके मकान का नंबर क्या है?
पंकज	–	नंबर तो मुझको याद नहीं है
कमल	–	अच्छा, कल बता दीजिए।
पंकज	–	उसका बड़ा-सा सफेद मकान है। उसके दरवाज पर पीपल का पेड़ है।
कमल	–	मैं ढूँढने की कोशिश करूंगा।
पंकज	–	उसके घर का फाटक हरा है।
कमल	–	अच्छा याद रखूँगा। आप भी मेरे साथ चलिए।
पंकज	–	हां, यह ठीक है। चलिए, मैं आपके साथ चलता हूँ।

Pankaj	—	*āp Rā ko jānate hain?*
Kamal	—	*jī nahīn, main nahīn janatā*
Pankaj	—	*vah āpke paros men rahtā hai.*
Kamal	—	*mujhako afsos hai ki main usase kabhi nahīn milā*

307

Pankaj —	*āp usase zarūr miliye. vah merā dso hai.*
Kamal —	*zarūr milūngā.*
Pankaj —	*Rām bahut dilchasp ādamī hai.*
Kamal —	*bahut achchī bāt hai.*
Pankaj —	*main Rām ko pichhale pandrah sala se jānatā hūm.*
Kamal —	*kyā āp sāth-sāth parhate the?*
Pankaj —	*jīhām, ham ek hīkaulij men parhte the.*
Kamal —	*kripā kar ke unakā patā dījiye. unake makān kā nambar kyā hai?*
Pankaj —	*nambar to mujhako yād nahīm hai.*
Kamal —	*achchhā, kal batā dījiye.*
Pankaj —	*usakā barāsā safed makān hai. usake darvāze par pipal kā per hai.*
Kamal —	*main dhūmdhane kī koshish karūngā*
Pankaj —	*usake ghar kā phāṭak harā hai.*
Kamal —	*achchhā yad rakhūngā. ap bhī mere sāth chaliye.*
Pankaj —	*hām, yah thīk hai. chaliye, main āpke sāth chalatā hūm.*

English Translation

Pankaj —	Do you know Ram?
Kamal —	No, I don't know.
Pankaj —	He lives in your neighbourhood.
Kamal —	I am soory that I have never met him.
Pankaj —	You meet him definitely. He is my friend.

Kamal	—	I shall definitely meet him.
Pankaj	—	Ram is a very interesting man.
Kamal	—	That's very good.
Pankaj	—	I have known Ram for the last fifteen years.
Kamal	—	Did you study together?
Pankaj	—	Yes, we studied in the same college.
Kamal	—	Please give me his address. What is his house number?
Pankaj	—	I don''t remember the number.
Kamal	—	Okay. Tell me tomorrow.
Pankaj	—	There is a big and white house. There is a pipul tree at the gate.
Kamal	—	I shall try to locate it.
Pankaj	—	The gate of his house is green.
Kamal	—	Okay. I shall remember it. Yoou come with me too.
Pankaj	—	That is right. Come, I shall come with you.

New Words

paros	neighbourhood	पड़ोस
janate hain	do you know	जानते है
mujhako afss hai	I am sorry	मुझको अफसोस है
kabhī nahīṁ	never	कभी नहीं
milā	met	मिला
dost	friend	दोस्त
dilshasp	interesting	दिलचस्प

pichhale	last, (bygone)	पिछले
sālon	years	सालों
sāth-sāth	together	साथ-साथ
ek hī	the same	एक ही
kripā kar ke	please, kindly	कृपा करके
patā	address	पता
dijīye	give	दीजिए
yād nahīm hai	don't remember	याद नहीं है
batā	tell	बता
pīpal	a kind of tree	पीपल
dhūmdhnā	search for	ढूंढना
koshish karūngā	shall try	कोशिश करूंगा
phātak	gate	फाटक
yād rakhūnga	shall remember	याद रखूँगा
mere sāth	with me	मेरे साथ

Reading Exercise V

कमल — आप कहाँ गए थे?

पंकज — मैं बाजार गया था।

कमल — आप कैसे गये थे? गाड़ी में?

पंकज — जी नहीं, मैं बस में गया था।

कमल — आपकी गाड़ी कहाँ है?

पंकज — गाड़ी खराब है, इसलिए मैं बस में गया।

कमल — आज दुकानें खुली है?

पंकज — जी हां, सब दुकानें खुली हैं।

कमल — मुझको परदे का कपड़ा खरीदना हैं।

पंकज — बाजार मेरे घर के पीछे ही है।

कमल — तो फिर आप बस में क्यों गए थे?

पंकज	–	मै तो सब्जी-मंडी गया था।
कमल	–	मेरे घर के सामने बाग है।
पंकज	–	शाम को बाग में बच्चे खेलेते हैं।
कमल	–	मेरे बच्चे घर के अन्दर ही खेलते है।
पंकज	–	उनको बाग में खेलना पसन्द नहीं हैं?
कमल	–	जी नहीं। अपने बच्चों को मेरे घार भेजिए।
पंकज	–	मैं आया तो बाहर का दरवाजा खुला था।
कमल	–	किसने खोला?
पंकज	–	मैं नहीं जानता। शायद नौकर ने खुला छोड़ दिया था।
कमल	–	नौकर बहुत लापरवाह है।
पंकज	–	आज कल बहुत चोरियां होती है।
कमल	–	लेकिन मेरा नौकर बिल्कुल नहीं समझता।

Kamal	–	*āp kahān gaye the?*
Pankaj	–	*main bāzār gayā thā.*
Kamal	–	*āp kaise gaye the? Gārī men?*
Pankaj	–	*jī nahīn, main bas men gayā thā.*
Kamal	–	*apkī garī kahān hai?*
Pankaj	–	*gārī kharāb hai isliye main bas men gayā.*
Kamal	–	*āj dūkanen khulī hain?*
Pankaj	–	*jī hān, sab dukāne khulīn hain.*
Kamal	–	*mujhako parde kā kaprā kharīdanā hai.*
Pankaj	–	*bāzār mere ghar ke pichhe hī hai.*
Kamal	–	*to phir āp bas men kyon gaye the?*
Pankaj	–	*main to sabzī mandī gayā thā.*
Kamal	–	*mere ghar ke sāmane bāg hai.*
Pankaj	–	*shām ko bāg men bachche khelate hain..*

Kamal	—	*mere bachche ghar ke andar hī khelate hain.*
Pankaj	—	*unko bāg men khelanā pasand nahīm hai?*
Kamal	—	*jī nahin. apne bachchon ko mere thar bhejiye.*
Pankaj	—	*main āyā to bāhar kā darvāzā khulā thā.*
Kamal	—	*kisane khola?*
Pankaj	—	*main nahin jānata. shāyad naukaar ne khulā chhor diya thā.*
Kamal	—	*naukar bahut lāparvah hai.*
Pankaj	—	*ājkal bahut choriyan hotī hain.*
Kamal	—	*lekin merā naukar bilkul nahīm samajhatā.*

New Words

gārī	car	गाड़ी
khulī	open	खुली
parde kā kaprā	curtain material	पर्दे का कपड़ा
ghar ke pichhe	behind the house	घर के पीछे
sabzī mandī	wholesale vegetable market	सब्जी मंडी
sāmne	in front	सामने
khelate hain	play	खेलते हैं
andar	inside	अन्दर
bhejiye	send	भेजिये
lāparvāh	careless	लापरवाह
choriyān	thefts	चोरियां
samajhate	understands	समझते

312

Reading Exercise VI

Where is the nearest barber?

Idhar sab se nazdīk kaun sā nāī hai?

इधर सबसे नजदीक कौन सा नाई है?

Can you give me a hair cut now?

Tum abhī mere bāl banā sakte ho?

तुम अभी मेरे बाल बना सकते हो?

When can you?

Kab banā sakoge?

कब बना सकोगे?

D I need an appoinment?

Wakt mukarrar kane kī zarūrat hai kyā?

वक्त मुकर्रर करने जरूरत है क्या?

Call the barber here.

Nāī ko idhar bulāo.

नाई को इधर बुलाओ।

Cut my hai please.

Mere bāl banā.

मेरे बाल बनाओ।

Not to short.

Bahut chhote nahīn.

बहुत छोटे नहीं।

Take off, only a little.

Bahut kam kato.

बहुत कम काटो।

Do not touch the top.

Ūpar ke bāl mat kāto.

ऊपर के बाल मत काटो।

313

Short at the sides.
Bājū wāle chhote karo.
बाजू वाले-छोटे करो।

Not so short in front.
Āge ki taraf itne chhote mat karo.
आगे की तरफ इतने छोटे मत करो।

A little shorter here.
Idhar se thore aur chhote karo
इधर से थोड़े और छोटे करो।

Leave that part alone.
Sirf voh hissā chhor do.
सिर्फ वो हिस्सा छोड़ दो।

Trim my beard slightly.
Merī darhī thorī-sī sanwāro.
मेरी दाढ़ी थोड़ी-सी संवारो।

Trim my moustache.
Merī mūchh sanwāro.
मेरी मूछँ संवारो।

Do it carefully.
Sāwdhānī se karo.
सावधानी से करो।

Please give me a shave. -
Merī dārhī banāo.
मेरी दाढ़ी बनाओ।

Shave me clean.
Ek dam sāf karo.
एक दम साफ करो।

Not so close.
Ultī mat karo—sambhlo.
उल्टी मत करो-संभलो।
Your razor is blunt.
Tumhārā ustarā kund hai.
तुम्हारा उस्तरा कुन्द है।
It Hurts.
Dard hotā hai
दर्द होता है।
Lather it more.
Zyādā sabun lagāo.
ज्यादा साबुन लगाओ।
Sharpen your razor.
Ustarā tez karo.
उस्तरा तेज करो।
Use clippers.
Machine se banāo.
मशीन से बनाओ।
Do not use clippers.
Machine se mat banao.
मशीन से बनाओ।
Do not use clippers.
Machine se mat banāo.
मशीन से मत बनाओ।
I prefer scissors.
Kanichī se banāo.
कैंची से बनाओ।

More off the neck.

Gardan ke bāl aur kāto.

गर्दन के बाल और काटो।

Give me a head massage.

Mere sir par mālish karo.

मेरे सिर पर मालिश करो।

I want a shampoo.

Sabun se mere bāl sāf karo.

साबुन से मेरे बाल साफ करो।

No hair oil please.

Balan men tel mat lagāo.

बालों में तेल मत लगाओ।

Part it here.

Idhar māng nikala.

इधर मांग निकालो।

I want my hair washed.

Mere bāl dha dālo.

मेरे बाल धो डालो।

I want a maincure.

Mujhe hath aur nākhūn ko sajane wālā chahiye.

मुझे हाथ और नाखून को सजने वाला चाहिए।

Can you give me a tint?

Tum rang lagā sakte ho?

तुम रंग लगा सकते हो।

Exercise VII

दिल्ली शहर की एक ही गली में दो आदमी रहते थे।
उनमें एक कन्जूस और दूसरा अमीर था। वे एक दूसरे
के पास आया जाया करते थे। और उनमें आपस में
दोस्ताना भी था। एक बार कन्जूस ने अमीर से कहा
कि: प्यारे दोस्त, मैं दूर दराज परदेश को जाता हूँ।
मैं तुम्हारी अंगूठी चाहता हूँ ताकि उसे देखकर मैं तुमको
याद करता रहूँ। अमीर ने जवाब दिया कि तुम अपनी
नन्ही उंगली को देख कर मुझे याद कर सकते हो।
असल दोस्ती को यादगार के लिए अंगूठी की जरूरत
नहीं है।

Delhi shhar ki ek hī galī men do ādmī rahe the.
Umen ek kanjūs aru dūsrā amīr thā. Ve ek dūsre
ke pās āyā jāyā karte the, aur unmen āpas men
dostānā bhī thā. Ek bār kanjūs ne amīr se kahā ki
Pyāre dost, main dūr darāj pradesh ko jātā hūm.
Main tumhārī angūthī chāhtā hūm tāki use dekh
kartā main tumko yād kartā rahūm. Amīr ne jawāb
diyā ki tum apnī nanhī unglī ko dekh kar mujhe
yād kar sakte ho. Asal dostī ko yādgār ke liye angūthī
kī jarūrāt nahīn hai.

English Translation

In a street in the city of Delhi lived two persons.
One was miser and the other was a rich man.

They used to visit one another and were on friendly terms. One day the miser said to the rich man: Dear friend, I am going to a far distant Country. I want your ring, so that by looking at it, I may constantly remember you. The rich man answered: When you see you bare finger. it will remined you of me. True friendship does not need rings and such like things for remembrance.

Chapter 45

Miscellaneous Exercise

I shall pay on receipt of the goods.
Māl āne par main dām dūngā.
माल आने पर में दाम दूंगा।

We have made every effort to execute your order.
Āp ke hukm bajāne men ham ne puri koshish kī hui.
आप के हुक्म बजाने में हम ने पूरी कोशिश की है।

Will you kindly let us know by return of post?
Kyā lautatī ḍāk se itla dene kī inayat karenge?
क्या लौटती डाक से इत्तला देने की इनायत करेंगे ?

Please accept our best thanks for this favour.
Is ināyat ke liye hamārā bahut shukriyā kabul kījiye.
इस इनायत के लिए हमारा बहुत शुक्रिया कबूल कीजिए।

There was a good trade done in that village.
Us gaon men achchhī tijārat hui.
उस गांव में अच्छी तिजारत है।

Our market is still very quiet.	Hamārā bāzār abhī bahut khāmosh hai.	हमारा बाजार अभी बहुत खामोश है।
There is little hope of an early change.	Jaldī badalne kī bahut kam ummīd hai.	जल्दी बदलने की बहुत कम उम्मीद है।
The demand is not yet strong enough.	Abhī mang kāfī nahīm hai.	अभी मांग काफी नहीं है।
We hope to obtain a better price in a week.	Ek hafte men ham behtar dām pāne kī ummīd karte bain.	एक हफ्ते में हम बेहतर दाम पाने की उम्मीद करते हैं।
Speculators have for the moment seized on this article.	Is vakt sattewālon ne is chīz par kabzā kar liyā hai.	इस वक्त सट्टेवालों ने इस चीज पर कब्जाकर लिया है।
Nobody can tell how the market will turn out.	Koī nahīm kah sakta kī bazar kī kyā hālat hogī.	कोई नहीं कह सकता कि बाजार की क्या हालत होगी।

320

If a considerable change takes place, we shall inform you by cable.	*Agar achchhā fark huā to hām ap ko tār se itlā denge*	अगर अच्छा फर्क हुआ तो हम आप को तार से इत्तला देंगे।
Prices will fall considerably in a few days.	*Kuchh dinon men dām bahut gir jāenge.*	कुछ दिनों में दाम बहुत गिर जाएंगे।
I like to read.	*Main parbnā pasand karatā hun.*	मैं पढ़ना पसंद करता हूँ।
He has written a new work.	*Usne ek nai pustak likhī hai.*	उसने एक नई पुस्तक लिखी है।
He is a government servant.	*Veh sarkarī naukar hai.*	वह सरकारी नौकर है।
The prince was present there.	*Veh rājkumar wvahan upsthit thā*	वह राजकुमार वहाँ उपस्थित था।
Come into my room.	*Mere kamre men āo.*	मेरे कमरे में आओ।

321

They will be married tomorrow.	Unkā byah kal hogā	उनका ब्याह कल होगा।
He has born before you.	Tumse pahle uskā janm huā thā	तुमसे पहले उसका जन्म हुआ था।
He has one son.	Uske ek betā hai.	उसके एक बेटा है।
Who lives there?	Wahan kaun rahtā hai?	वहाँ कौन रहता है?
When did he come?	Veh kab āyā	वह कब आया?
When will you go again?	Tum kab phir jāoge?	तुम कब फिर जाओगे?
You must not beat her.	Tumhen usko mārnā nahīn chāhiye.	तुम्हें उसको मारना नहीं चाहिए।
I want to speak to you.	Main tumse kuchh bāt-chīt karna chāhtā hun.	मैं तुमसे कुछ बात-चीत करना चाहता हूँ।
I am displeased with you.	Main tumse aprasann hun.	मैं तुमसे अप्रसन्न हूँ।

322

Do not disappoint me.	*Mujhe nirash mat karo.*	मुझे निराश मत करो।
I shall take rest.	*Main ārām karungā*	मैं आराम करूँगा।
Is the air cool?	*Hawā thandī hai?*	हवा ठंडी है?
Come after dinner.	*Bhojan ke bād āo.*	भोजन के बाद आओ।
He wants you.	*Veh tumhe bulā rahā hai*	वह तुम्हें बुला रहा है।
London is bigger than Bombay.	*London bombai se barā hai.*	लंदन बम्बई से बड़ा है।
London is the biggest of all.	*London sab-se barā hai*	लंदन सब से बड़ा है।
Is this your house?	*Yah tumhārā ghar hai?*	यह तुम्हारा घर है?
What will you eat?	*Āp kya khaenge?*	आप क्या खाएँगे?
Who has done this?	*Yah kis-ne kiyā hai?*	यह किस ने किया है?

323

What is your order?	*Āpki agya kya hai?*	आपकी आज्ञा क्या है ?
Are you at leisure?	*Tumko awakash hai?*	तुमको अवकाश है ?
Is this the very thing?	*Kyā yeh vahī hai?*	क्या यह वही है ?
He is a fool.	*Veh murkh hai.*	वह मूर्ख है।
Go, you have leave.	*Chale jāō, tumko chutti hai.*	चले जाओ, तुमको छुट्टी है।
Send them to my house.	*Unko mere ghar bhej-do.*	उनको मेरे घर भेज दो।
He is a drunkard	*Veh sharaābi hai.*	वह शराबी है।
What is your advice?	*Tumhāri kyā rāy hai?*	तुम्हारी क्या राय है ?
What is the fare for a day?	*Ek din ka bhara kyā hai?*	एक दिन का क्या भाड़ा है ?
This rupee is counterfeit.	*Yah rupiyā khotā hai*	यह रुपया खोटा है।
Who is the owner of this house?	*Is ghar kā mālik kaun hain?*	इस घर का मालिक कौन है ?

324

He has no money.	Uske pās paisā nahīṃ hai.	उसके पास पैसा नहीं है।
I received your letter just now.	Mujhe tumharī chitthī abhī milī.	मुझे तुम्हारी चिट्ठी अभी मिली।
He is ready to go.	Veh jāne ko taiyār hai.	वह जाने को तैयार है।
He has finished his work.	Veh kam kār chukā hai.	वह काम कर चुका है।
Ask him his name.	Us-se puchho ki-uskā nām kyā hai.	उससे पूछो कि उसका नाम क्या है।
Burn these waste papers.	Yah raddi kagaz jalā do.	यह रद्दी कागज जला दो।
He has come on business.	Veh kām ke-liye āyā hai.	वह काम के लिये आया है।
Throw away this clothing.	Yah kaprā phenk do.	यह कपड़ा फेंक दो।
Wait a little he is putting on clothes.	Zara thahro, woh kapra pahantā hai.	जरा ठहरो, वह कपड़े पहनता है।

He always drives very fast.	Veh apnī gāṛī sadā tez chalātā hai.	वह अपनी गाड़ी सदा तेज चलाता है।
Who is that person?	Veh vyakti kaun hai?	यह व्यक्ति कौन है?
Shut your eyes.	Ānkhen mincho.	आखें मींचो।
Do you know the cause of it?	Tum is-ka kāran jānte ho?	तुम इसका कारण जानते हो?
I said nothing.	Main kuchh nahīn bolā	मैं कुछ नहीं बोला।
What you say is all true.	Jo tum kahte ho sab sach hai.	जो तुम कहते हो सब सच है।
Sir, it is not my fault.	Mahashaya, mera dosh nahīn hai.	महाशय मेरा दोष नहीं है।
I am fond of hunting.	Mujhe shikār kā shauk hai.	मुझे शिकार का शौक है।
We walk about the city.	Ham log shahar mein ghumte hain.	हम लोग शहर में घूमते हैं।

I hope that.....

Mujhe ashā hai ki.....

मुझे आशा है कि

That merchant is very rich.

Veh wyapari barā dhanwān hai.

वह व्यापारी बड़ा धनवान है।

I have 400 rupees.

Mere pās chār sau rupiye hain.

मेरे पास चार सौ रुपये हैं।

Give them two rupees each.

Unke do do rupiye do.

उनको दो-दो रुपये दो।

Look at that man.

Us manushya ko dekho.

उस मनुष्य को देखो।

Take a little walk in the garden.

Bāgh men zarā tahlo.

बाग में ज़रा टहलो।

This type of fruit is plentiful here.

Is prakār ke phal yahan bahut hain.

इस प्रकार के फल यहां बहुत है।

Sow this seed here.

Is bīj ko idhar bo-o.

इस बीज को इधर बोओ।

He wears spectacles.

Veh ainak lagāā hai.

वह ऐनक लगाता है।

English	Transliteration	Devanagari
I cannot assist you.	Main tumh $\bar{a}$ $r\bar{a}$ $b\bar{a}$ h nahin bat $\bar{a}$ sakt $\bar{a}$	मैं तुम्हारा हाथ नहीं बटा सकता।
The war will last about three years.	Lagbhag t $\bar{n}$ baras tak yudb jar $\bar{i}$ rahega	लगभग तीन बरस तक युद्ध जारी रहेगा।
The allies will get success.	Mitron k $\bar{i}$ jit bog $\bar{i}$.	मित्रों की जीत होगी।
Thank God, I am quite well.	Iswar k $\bar{i}$ kripa se main babut acbchh $\bar{a}$ hun.	ईश्वर की कृपा से मैं बहुत अच्छा हूँ।
The time is over.	Samay ho ch $\bar{u}$ ka.	समय हो चुका
I am very glad to see you.	$\bar{A}$ pko dekb-kar mujhe bad $\bar{a}$ harsb hot $\bar{a}$ hai	आपको देखकर मुझे बड़ा हर्ष होता है।
What did you say?	$\bar{A}$ pne kya kah $\bar{a}$?	आपने क्या कहा ?
I am afraid.	Mujhe dar bai	मुझे डर है।

328

I thank you.	Main tumhen dhanyawād detā hun.	मैं तुम्हें धन्यवाद देता हूँ।
I have heard nothing.	Main ne kuchh nahīn sunā hai.	मैंने कुछ नहीं सुना है।
He has many friends.	Uske anek mitar hain.	उसके अनेक मित्र हैं।
He demanded ten rupees.	Usne das rupiye mange.	उसने दस रुपए मांगे।
Lock up the box.	Petī kā tālā lagāo.	पेटी का ताला लगाओ।
Put a Rupee stamp on this letter.	Is chitthī par ek āne kā tikat lagāo.	इस चिट्ठी पर एक आने का टिकट लगाओ।
Are your parents alive?	Tumhāre mā-bap jīvit hain?	तुम्हारे मां-बाप जीवित है?
I shall punish him.	Main use dand dungā.	मैं उसे दंड दूँगा।
Why did you abuse him?	Tum ne kyon use galī dī?	तुमने क्यों उसे गाली दी?

English	Transliteration	Devanagari
There was a fire in the bazar last night.	*Gai-rāt bazar men āg lagī thī.*	गई रात बाज़ार में आग लगी थी।
It was soon put out.	*Usko jaldī bujhā diyā.*	उसको जल्दी बुझा दिया।
Do you know who set it on fire?	*Tum jante ho āg kisne lagāī?*	तुम जानते हो आग किसने लगाई?
Why did you not ask leave?	*Tumne chutti kyon na lī?*	तुमने छुट्टी क्यों न ली?
He is a regular thief.	*Veh pakkā chor hai.*	वह पक्का चोर है।
Tell him to be careful in future.	*Usse kaho ki bhavishya mein sajag raho.*	उससे कहो कि भविष्य में सजग रहो।
How far is the city from here?	*Yahan se shahar kitnī dur hai?*	यहाँ से शहर कितनी दूर है ?
I waited for you a long time.	*Bahut der tak main ne tumharī rah dekhī.*	बहुत देर तक मैंने तुम्हारी राह देखी।

He has gone to Europe on leave.	*Wah chhutti par wilāyat gayā hai.*	वह छुट्टी पर विलायत गया है।
What is the good of that?	*Us-se kya labh hai?*	उससे क्या लाभ है?
Where did you hear this news?	*Tum ne yah samachar kahan sunā?*	तुमने यह समाचार कहाँ सुना?
We are certain that you will be satisfied with the quality and price.	*Hamen yakīn hai ki āp chiz aur dam se khush honge.*	हमें यकीन है कि आप चीज और दाम से खुश होंगे।
We await your acknowldgement of the receipt.	*Ham rasīd kī pahunch ka intizar kar rahe hain.*	हम रसीद की पहुँच का इन्तजार कर रहे हैं।
The goods invoiced on the 17th inst. have arrived here to-day	*Sattrah tarikh ko jis māl ki bilti bheji gayi thi veh āj a gayi.*	सत्रह तारीख को जिस माल की बिल्टी भेजी गई थी वह आज आ गई।

Unfortunately they are in such a bad condition that we cannot accept them.	*Badkismati se wah itnī kharab halat men hai ki ham manzur nahīn kar sakte.*	बदकिस्मती से वह इतनी खराब हालत में है। कि हम मंजूर नहीं कर सकते।
Will you let us know what we can do for you in this matter?	*Kyā āp hamen batayengeki is mamle men ham ap ke liye kyā kar sakte hain?*	क्या आप हमें बताएंगे कि इस मामले में हम आप के लिये क्या कर सकते हैं?
We beg to inform you that the cotton sales have been in progress for a week.	*Ham āp ko itla dete hain ke rui ki farokht kīek hafte se ho rahī hai.*	हम आप को इतला देते है कि रूई की फरोख्त एक हफ्ते से हो रही है।
We advise you to buy now (at once).	*Ham āpko salāh dete hain ki āp fauran hi kharīden.*	हम आप को सलाह देते है कि आप फौरन ही खरीदें।
The terms quoted do not include carriage.	*Is bhav men bhejne kā kharch nahīn shamil hai.*	इस भाव में भेजने का खर्च नहीं शामिल है।

The firm has been established for many years.	Yah kārkbānā muddat se kāyam hai.	यह कारखाना मुद्दत से कायम है।
The bill of lading has not yet come to hand.	Lādne ka bil abhi nahīṁ āyā hai.	लादने का बिल अभी नहीं आया है।
A waiting the favour of a reply	Jawāb kī meherbani ka intizār hai.	जवाब की मेहरबानी का इन्तजार है।
The money marked is very firm.	Rupaye kā bazar bahut mazboot bai.	रुपए का बाजार बहुत मजबूत है।
We must be prepared for still dearer money.	Is se bhi mehenge rupaye ke liye hamen taiyar rahanā chāhiye.	इस से भी मंहगे रुपए के लिए हमें तैयार रहना चाहिए।
The value of the rice and wheat exported last week, amounted to half a million	Akhiri hafte bahar bheje .buye chāval aur gehun kī kīmat pable bafte ke	आखिरी हफ्ते बाहर भेजे हुए चावल और गेहूँ की कीमत पहले हफ्ते की बनिस्बत

English	Transliteration	Devanagari
rupees more than the previous week.	*banisbat panch lākh rupaye zyada thī.*	पाँच लाख रुपए ज्यादा थी।
It is essential to ship the goods at the lowest possible rate.	*Yah nihāyat zaruri hai ki mal kam se kam dar par jahaz se bhejā jāye.*	यह निहायत जरूरी है कि माल कम से कम दर पर जहाज से भेजा जाए।
The date of the arrival does not matter much.	*Amad kī tarikh ki koi bat nabīn.*	आमद की तारीख की कोई बात नहीं।
Do not forget to insure the goods.	*Māl ka bimā karanā mat bhulnā*	माल की बीमा करना मत भूलना।
We think there will shortly be a very great demand for cotton in this country.	*Hamārā khhyal hai ki kuchh din men hi is mulk men rui ki bari mang hogī.*	हमारा ख्याल है कि कुछ दिन में ही इस मुल्क में रूई की बड़ी मांग होगी।
Our present supply will not be sufficient to meet the demand.	*Hamārā maujudā sāmān hamara mang ke liye kaafī na hogā.*	हमारा मौजूदा सामान माँग के लिए काफी न होगा।

We propose entering into another speculation with you, on equal terms.	हमारा इरादा है कि आप के साथ बराबर हिस्सों में एक और सट्टा करें।	Hamārā irādā hai ki āp ke sath barabar bisson men ek aur sattā karen.
We herewith send you invoice for goods ordered on the 5th inst.	पांचवीं तारीख को मंगवाये हुए माल की बिल्टी हम भेजते हैं।	Panchvi tārīkh komangvaye huyemal ki bilti ham bhejte hain.
We are sending them off by ship to-day.	हम आज उन्हें जहाज से रवाना कर रहे हैं।	Ham aj unhen jahhaz se ravānā kar rahe hain.
Where can I buy those articles (things)?	वे चीजें मैं कहां खरीद सकता हूँ?	Ve chizen main kahan kharid saktā hun?
To whom to these parcels belong?	ये पार्सल किस के हैं?	Ye pārsal kis key hain?
Is he any relative of yours?	क्या वह तुम्हारा रिश्तेदार है?	Kyā wah tumhārā rishtedar hai?

335

What are you doing here?	तुम यहाँ क्या कर रहे हो?	*Tum yahan kyā kar rahe ho?*
I know what I have to do.	मैं जानता हूँ कि मुझे क्या करना है	*Main jāntā hun ki mujhe kya karnā hai.*
I understand you quite well.	मैं तुम्हें ठीक-ठाक समझता हूँ	*Main tumhen thik thāk samajhtā hun.*
Now I know what to say.	अब मैं जानता हूँ कि क्या कहूँ	*Ab main jāntā hun ki kya kahun.*
Someone must do it.	किसी न किसी को यह करना चाहिए	*Kisi na kisi ko yah karnā chāhiye.*
I believe there is no one at home.	मेरा यकीन है कि घर पर कोई नहीं है	*Mere yakin hai ki ghar par koi nahin hai.*

336

He must have about three hundred rupees in hand.

Uske pās karib tīn sau rupaye honge.

उसके पास करीब तीन सौ रुपए होंगे।

There were about two hundred persons present.

Koī do sau ādmi maujud the.

कोई दो सौ आदमी मौजूद थे।

Some house or other must be vacant.

Koi na koi makān zarur khali bogā

कोई न कोई मकान जरूर खाली होगा।

This house compared with that house, is the more beautiful.

Us ghar ke mukabile yah ghar zyadā khubsurat hai.

उस घर के मुकाबले यह घर ज्यादा खूबसूरत है।

These two books are quite different.

Ye do kitāben bilkul mukhtalifhain.

ये दो किताबें बिल्कुल मुख्तलिफ हैं।

One is much larger than the other.

Ek dusri se babut barīhai.

एक दूसरी से बहुत बड़ी है।

English	Transliteration	Devanagari
Go, otherwise you will catch cold.	*Jao, nahīṃ-to tumko sardi hogī.*	जाओ, नहीं तो तुमको सर्दी होगी।
We know it all.	*Ham yah sab jānte hain.*	हम यह सब जानते हैं।
Hang up this lamp	*Yah battī latkā do.*	यह बत्ती लटका दो।
It is very late, let us go home.	*bahut der hui, chalo hum ghar chalen.*	बहुत देर हुई, चलो हम घर चलें।
You go on, we are coming.	*Tum āge jāo, ham pichhe ā rahe hain.*	तुम आगे जाओ, हम पीछे आ रहे हैं।
Does the climate of this place agree with you?	*Yahan kī āb-o-hawā tumhare anukul hai?*	यहाँ की आबो-हवा तुम्हारे अनुकूल है?
This depends upon you.	*Yah āp par nirbhar hai.*	यह आप पर निर्भर है।
Have you ever been to Delhi?	*Āp kabhī Delhi gaye hain?*	आप कभी दिल्ली गए हैं?
I do not know him.	*Man usko nahīṃ pahchāntā*	मैं उसको नहीं पहचानता।

Can you write?	*Tum likh-sakte ho?*	तुम लिख सकते हो ?
He beat his wife.	*Usne apnī patnī ko marā.*	उसने अपनी पत्नी को मारा।
How long have you been in India?	*Āp kitne din se Hindustān men bain?*	आप कितने दिन से हिन्दुस्तान में है ?
What is your intention?	*Tumharā āshay kyā hai?*	तुम्हारा आशय क्या है ?
Send for him quickly	*Use jaldi bulā-bhejo.*	उसे जल्दी बुला - भेजो।
How you came to know that?	*Tumne use kaise jān liyā?*	तुमने उसे कैसे जान लिया ?
Change the water daily.	*Pratidin pānī badlo.*	प्रतिदिन पानी बदलो।
Take the rubbish away.	*Yah kura karkat le jāo.*	यह कूड़ा करकट ले जाओ।
What does it resemble?	*Yah kis se miltā hai?*	यह किस से मिलता है ?
I shall fine You.	*Main tumben dand karunga.*	मैं तुम्हें दण्ड करूंगा।
Let him go out.	*Usko bāhar jane-do.*	उसको बाहर जाने दो।
Let him come in.	*Usko andar āne-do.*	उसको अन्दर आने दो।

339

Do it to-day instead of tomorrow.	*Kal ke badle aāj karo.*	कल के बदले आज करो।
Where does Mr. Bell live?	*Bell mahashay kahan rahte hain?*	बेल महाशय कहाँ रहते हैं ?
This book is very good.	*Yah pustak bahut achchhī hai.*	यह पुस्तक बहुत अच्छी है।
What is the name of your wife?	*Tumhari patni kā nām kyā hai?*	तुम्हारी पत्नी का नाम क्या है ?
Where were you yesterday?	*Kal tum kahan the?*	कल तुम कहां थे ?
What is this thing?	*Yah chīz kyā hai?*	यह चीज़ क्या है ?
Who are these people?	*Yah kaun log hain?*	यह कौन लोग है ?
My friend lives with me.	*Mer āmitra mere sāth rahtā hai.*	मेरा मित्र मेरे साथ रहता है।
What did you eat to day?	*Āaj tum ne kyā khayā?*	आज तुम ने क्या खाया?
What can you do?	*Tum kyā kar-sakte ho?*	तुम क्या कर सकते हो ?

340

Stock Phrases for Greetings Telegrams

In English	In Hindi
1. My heartiest Diwali Greetings to you.	दीपावली की हार्दिक शुभ कामनाएं।
2. Id mubarak.	ईद मुबारिक।
3. Heartiest Vijaya greetings.	विजया की हार्दिक शुभ कामनाएं।
4. A happy new year to you.	नव वर्ष आपको शुभ हो।
5. Many happy returns of the day.	ईश्वर करे यह शुभ दिन बार-बार आये।
6. Best congratulations new arrival.	पुत्र-जन्म पर हार्दिक बधाई।
7. Congratulations on the distinction conferred on you.	आप को इस सम्मान पर हार्दिक बधाई।
8. Best wishes for a long and happy married life.	सुखमय और चिरस्थायी वैवाहिक जीवन के लिये हमारी शुभ कामनाएँ।
9. A merry Christmas to you.	क्रिसमिस की हार्दिक शुभकामनाएँ।
10. Hearty congratulations on your success in the examination.	परीक्षा में सफलता पर हार्दिक बधाई।

11. Best wishes for a safe and pleasant Journey. आपकी यह यात्रा आनन्दमय और सकुशल हा।

12. Hearty congratulations on the success in election. चुनाव में सफलता पर हार्दिक बधाई

13. Many thanks for your good wishes which I/we reciprocate most heartily. आपकी शुभ कामनाओं के लिए। कोटिशः धन्यवाद।

14. Congratulations. बधाई।

15. Loving Greetings सप्रेम शुभकामनाएं

16. May Heaven's choicest blessings be showered on the young couple नव दम्पत्ति पर परमात्मा की असीम कृपा हो।

17. Wish you both a happy and prosperous wedded life आप दोनों का दाम्पत्य जीवन सुखी तथा समृद्धिशाली हो।

18. Kind rememberances and all good wishes for the Independence Day स्वतन्त्रता दिवस पर मंगल कामनाएँ।

19. Sincere Greetings for the Republic Day. Long live the Republic हार्दिक बधाई 'अमर रहे जन तन्त्र हमारा'।

20. My heartiest Holi greetings to you. होली की शुभकामनाएँ।